Preface

I love hiking. More accurately, I really enjoy it and spend an incredible amount of my spare time hiking in a lot of different places throughout Arizona. Now, I don't mind the kind of hiking that includes trails and other people, but most of my hiking does not. I like to walk into the middle of nowhere looking for stuff. I search for adventures, fallen antlers, geodes, and whatever other treasures that have been left behind. Even if the trip includes others, we split up and I spend a lot of time walking alone on my hikes.

As a currently single, non-parent, becoming more and more of an introverted type of person, I have some free time that some others do not. I also intentionally make the time that others do not. The older I get, the more value I have learned to give time. I really try not to waste it. During this time, walking through the woods, I have had the weirdest of conversations with myself. I have intentionally spent the time to pay attention to my thoughts, not wrapped up in the ever more relaxing downtime habit, I call, phoning. This of course is simply the adjective form of using your phone, but for everything except calling someone. I will try not to go on and on about the negative consequences of phones becoming a recreational past time, but it is incredibly relevant to the recovery of a teacher, therefore important. So, it will be mentioned a few times.

You would have to put your phone down to notice, but look around you. Far beyond calling and texting, those little devices are taking over in places they do not belong. People are using phones everywhere, in ways so unnecessary, habitually wasting so many moments of the day. People even use their phones while they workout at the gym. Trust me, I am often waiting on them while they waste so much time scrolling in between sets. These folks have stronger thumbs and pointer fingers than any other muscle group.

I have caught myself, along with many others on their phones, while "watching" tv. If we are so bored with whatever we are watching, then change the channel. Don't add another stimulant... multi-task screening, I guess. Even on the road, many drivers have one hand on the wheel and one hand holding the phone. Families sitting at dinner, avoiding eye contact and real conversations, staring into their screens is one of the saddest consequences from the phone.

Phones don't only distract us from the obvious things mentioned above. Phones become a type of crutch. When a person should learn how to get somewhere by watching the road, instead they rely on GPS. Instead of suffering to recall a little relevant fact in a conversation, we look it up to satisfy, prove others wrong, or prove ourselves right. Rather than teaching a child self-control, we hand them a phone to avoid a fit and public embarrassment. We further handicap ourselves with phones in too many ways to mention here.

The more I stepped away from the phone on my hikes, the more I looked at how people use it as a serious sickness. I saw how it was specifically hurting me and really holding me back. It distracted me from part of my recovery as a teacher, but only for a while. The phone is simply a misused tool, *a terribly misused tool*! I mention it here because it may be a critical part of breaking away from your own self-inflicted patterns.

Out in the woods, most of the time the phone service does not exist. Many times, I have it turned off anyway. Somewhere in the middle of nowhere, with no phone in hand, there is nowhere to run from the thoughts that hide in one's head. Without the phone, there is no social media to save me from personal attacks, repeating self-doubts, or past disappointments.

I have started to spend so much time hiking like this that I am very aware of my thoughts out there, maybe too much sometimes. But it turns out to be quite simple... If you just slow down, sometimes stop everything, and give yourself a break from the regular - you can find something else. I had to do this breakaway frequently to start finding a way out of my own negative patterns.

I noticed other patterns in my thoughts, not only the bad ones. Positive patterns with negative consequences. Growth and avoidance patterns. I had to deal with some demons hidden in there too. As I walked and thought, I found simple solutions to most of the problems. I started to learn from my past mistakes, now that I took the time to see them. I worked hard to try to become a better person, by recognizing what patterns helped me - verse hurt me.

After I worked hard on myself, I couldn't help but look at others' patterns. I thought about what my family and friends were going through and started to learn from their mistakes too. One learns quickly from their own mistakes, especially when they take the time to notice and admit them. One learns much more quickly when they combine this self-vulnerability with less judgment of others' behaviors. It is much too easy to miss all life's lessons when our eyes are clouded with judgment. Do not use other people's patterns against them, to put them down, or to feel better about yourself. Instead, use other's negative patterns for your own positive change. This way, we learn from others' mistakes too. I really put some serious effort into trying to change my thinking; change who I was a little bit. I wasn't a terrible person, I just wanted to be better.

Intentionally spending this time on these hikes, away from all the distractions of life, is what allowed me to finally take captive of all the thoughts that can be overlooked by a person. This mindful approach, to thinking about what was in my head on the hikes, showed more and more patterns. I thought of old and new relationships. I thought of anything from stupid to fantastic song lyrics. I pondered life itself for goodness' sake; whatever that means... I thought about so many things, but there was one thing that would never leave me alone.

I always thought about work. No matter how hard I tried, I couldn't escape thinking about what I didn't get done or a new idea for a lesson the following week. The students' and staff problems followed me into the woods too. I would worry about upcoming meetings; plan exactly what to do and say. So much of the week was filled with it, so work was heavy on the mind. Of course, other thoughts popped into the old noggin occasionally, but the patterns were always dominated by work. I thought about working way too much.

Intro

It was only when I began to practice what I am about to preach to you that I realized how true this idea can be. When I stopped ruining myself at work by doing everything I was asked, I had more time to see it and eventually feel it. I had to stop what I had done for so long in my teaching career; I stopped showing up early and staying late after work. I stopped trying to please all my colleagues with all their expectations. I stopped doing all the extra stuff that, at the time, made me the best damn teacher out there. I don't mean to brag, but I have the employee of the month, cheaply printed pieces of paper, to prove it. LOL

My coworkers and every other teacher friend of mine continued to complain daily about the extra stuff they were still doing, while I just stopped. My teaching friends didn't have time to hang out after work because they were catching up on grading and lesson plans. I refused to catch up and went to walk alone in the woods. I made a commitment to not take anything from work home with me. (This became easier over time because I started working in a contracted position, not trapped within the insatiable district standards) Starting with my computer, I just stopped bringing all that stuff home.

Here I was dipping my toe into this whole new world with a freedom I had never felt since working as a teacher. I started to have more and more free time, but anyone that could relate to what I was trying - was too busy to talk about it. My work friends were still busy with stupid schoolwork. It was nearly impossible to line up with my brothers' weird work schedules. My sister was too busy working overnights to do anything during regular human being hours. Even my 70-year-old mother was so busy working that she didn't have the energy to hang out. I was all alone in this new freedom from work, no one to share it with. I was trying to figure something out and break some long-lasting habits, basically by myself.

Work effort is a hard habit to break. I learned it from that 70-year-old mother previously mentioned. She was a single mother of 4, always working hard to keep us going. She often had multiple jobs, with too much to do and crazy hours. At that point, she really had to. My mom taught me how to work hard through many real-life examples. She doesn't need to work anymore; she just can't stop. She is programmed like so many of us. It is the same reason my friends, sister and so many others work the same way. I seem to have the same problem. And it is a problem.

It is a common problem for many good teachers. Somehow the best teachers are always giving, empathetic, hardworking, people pleasing types. To stop these patterns of mine at work has taken me an incredible effort, that I am still practicing. Don't confuse things early off here. I am still on time every day. I am still present at the meetings I need to be a part of. I still work my ass off for the students every day with a smile. I am still the one of the hardest working, "favorite teachers" on campus.

The difference is, I am learning a way to do less of the extra work with more joy left for other things. I am starting to recognize what I can say no to and who I can say no to. I will not embrace the circus act any longer and certainly don't want to be anywhere near a ringleader. I climbed that ladder, jumped through those hoops, and didn't like what I found up there. The biggest difference in my teaching career now is that I have taken control.

I am starting to feel less stuck, more in charge of my own career. In a career that can be so strangely exaggerated as complicated, I am finding simplicity. In a field where so many burn out, I am a steady flame. Most important, I see what I couldn't see because I was too close, wrapped up in work. I am learning that success, for me, isn't going to be found at work.

With clarity, I can think back to how much wasted time I have spent "behind the desk" at home. I am done with it. There is a piece of me coming back that has been in the dark for much too long. It is a piece of me that hasn't gotten enough light to grow. The big difference is, I am growing in life much more intentionally by not allowing work to get in the way.

This new idea that I have been experimenting with is working for me. It is working so well that I often walk around my current workplace with a smile. Other teachers have noticed too. I intentionally started making the time to share some of my ideas with my stressed-out coworkers. Over the last couple years, I spoke with so many teachers as I learned the ins and outs of every copy machine out there. Most of them started the conversations unknowingly, while they complained about this and that. I respectfully listened and recognized the patterns. Many of the same complaints they gave me were the same work "obligations" I have given up. Many of the excuses they gave for working so hard echoed from my adventures in the woods. I had worked hard to fight off those patterns for me. Now it was time to try the same for others.

No matter how many people agree or feel similar in the workplace, I still know this book will not reach some teachers. Just like at school, people will embrace the idea around the copy machine but not have the boldness to change. Like many other areas in life, it is easier to live the lies than to find the truth.

The information in this book will be controversial in some ways, readily rejected by those set in their teaching habits, *influenced strongly from a culture promoting career success over any other*. Some of the topics brought up in this book will not be heard, simply because some people do not want to hear anything different from what they already know. It's more comfortable to stay on the well-defined trail for most folks. On top of all that, the message may be missed because people just don't read anymore. LOL

If you do find yourself reading this, the following ideas are simply some suggestions. There are no solid guidelines to offer you the same peace of mind I am finding as a recovering teacher. However, some of the key ideas can make it easier for you to set up your own curriculum and standards in how you want to recover as a teacher. I may even offer some personally used accommodations and modifications to support your journey. The message might just help you figure it out sooner than I did. When I started writing this book, I didn't have any guidelines in mind. They just kind of developed as I practiced the idea. These ideas are still developing, as I continue through the many blunders along a teacher's path.

Eventually, I found a purpose in this writing too, no matter how hidden in my terrible analogies. The purpose of this book is not to detour anyone from teaching; it is not to highlight teaching as any harder or more stressful than any other job. This book, also, is not meant to complain about political ignorance, along with poor leadership that drives the decisions made in so many schools. Though it will be referenced. A magnificent revolution is not the intent of this writing. Furthermore, this book is not meant for teachers who are unable to work on their own faults, so distracted they don't even see them. This book will not reach people who are programmed by other's decisions, their phones, their own ego, etc. The message will go right over the heads of those blindly following their own bad habits or whoever is in "charge".

This book is meant for teachers who want something different for themselves. The type of people with a growth mindset, not filled with excuses. The words are specifically set up to relate with all the teachers I have spoken with over the last years. This book has been written for me and for teachers who may need to hear that there is a better, or at least a different, way. There is a version of teachers walking into their school with ease, energy, desire, and outstanding confidence. They even leave work feeling the same way. There are teachers out there that make a difference in their friends and family's lives, just as much as with students at their jobs. A few simple changes in daily practices may help teachers learn the importance and the 'how to' of recovering as a teacher.

This writing will tell the story of all teachers; the teachers that made it through, the teachers that gave up, the teachers that are trying to decide. There is no doubt in my mind that the themes brought up throughout this book ring true in many professions beyond just teaching. In fact, the more I wrote, the more I realized these problems could be in every single job out there. This writing is meant to inspire in any direction that anyone needs, along with providing a way to get there.

In this book, the word teacher refers to our wonderful cross-guards, the ladies in the front office, and the custodians stuck cleaning up another vandalism in the boy's bathroom. It also includes the cafeteria staff serving those fantastic sloppy joes. With extra highlight, this book uses the word teacher to include the paraprofessionals that often teach just as much as the lead teacher. Those fantastic school nurses must be included in this as well. Hang out in a nurse's office and you will learn anything from stopping a nosebleed to how to properly stab a kid with an Epi pen. The word teacher also includes the social workers, the clinical staff, speech and OT services for sure. An Occupational Therapy room can be one hell of a fun place to hang out. Bus drivers, coaches, and any other position I have forgotten are a part of what makes up the teaching world. Of course, we must include those typical old school room teachers too.

This book's concepts are based on opinions combined with evident truths, even if they are ignored. The words are guided by experience and new learned confidence to do things differently than how so many others have decided to take on the teaching career. These ideas are not up to debate in this author's life; not anymore. I am living it to prove it to myself; it is working! The educational proverbs coming from this writing are a commitment to a new way to be a teacher; a new way to look at work, combined with a new outlook on life.

I included some statistics and research into this writing along the way. I did it to try and validate some claims for you arguing type folks out there. Also, I thought it might make me sound smarter. LOL The further I went into the stats and research; I realized it was bringing me away from the point. Though there were many claims I could have used to support this writing, easily guided by a bias search on google, I chose to use fewer to focus on feelings. I wanted to focus on the patterns of feelings that all those struggling teachers had shared with me. The goal - to echo their words, ideas, and thoughts without all the extra rhetoric. I wanted to try to share honestly and openly how I personally felt throughout the ride. I wanted to write about all the things that are not put into statistical studies. A little bit of the qualitative over the quantitative, no matter how hard that is to express to others.

Besides, everyone knows statistics are paid for, can easily be skewed, and are often wrong. There are just too many factors that are left out of most studies. On top of that, there are too many errors by those creating the stats. If you didn't know that yet, now you do. Go ahead and look it up on your phone to find me at error, I know you want to. They're called statistical fallacies. Statistics can often be a bunch of bullshit. Try not to get hung up on the numbers is my point.

Fudging numbers is exactly the case in schools. Late parents do it by speeding to the school they gave a fake address - to get their kid into. Students do it by cheating on their least favorite subject. Teachers do it in the classroom to make their scores look good. Principals make up the craziest numbers or just repeat what they were told by the school board. Districts fudge numbers with all sorts of things for state or federal funding. Charter schools may have invented their own new math to do the things they do, something with imaginary numbers. LOL Special education teachers might not even know how to do math, according to the progress reports and caseloads given by case managers over the years. Anyone with their own eyes to look through has seen the misuse of numbers within a school.

You can listen to the few puppets on top who say what they are told. You can repeat a bunch of numbers made up from a guy who has not been in school since he was a child. Or, like my mother, you could listen to the recent national news to find out what drama, trauma, or tragedy is happening in schools that week.

There is a whole lot of misinformation put out from too many sources to keep up with. *From my point of view, right in the middle of the teaching world. That misinformation is terribly effective, but in the wrong direction.* From my advantage point, it is almost like it is done on purpose to keep people distracted. I am no longer following the sleight of hand. I have chosen to spend more time in the trenches to share a more real experience. I am trying my best to repeat what so many teachers have shared with me that they would not do anything about. I am refusing to listen to the types of leaders that have taken me down too many wrong paths.

I have no statistics to back this up, but I can make some up like the best of them. I would say that about 10% of you have figured out the message in this book already, or think you have. Part of this 10% will look at this book as an obvious observation and the other part will learn from this book how to share the idea with others. Part of that 10% also work in totally different industries now and make much more money. LOL. On the other hand, 90% of teachers have no idea how to recover. Some of these 90% may not even see the need or are so overwhelmed, they have never had the time to think about it. Many are lost in the patterns, simply doing what they're told, making jokes about it to get through. I think a large part of the 90% simply need to step away to see a little bit clearer. All the statistical bullshit aside, my hope is that some of you will find something in this book that prevents burning out and sparks a recovery of your own.

Chapter 1 – Recovering Teacher

I remember exactly where I was, the seat at the bar, the few people around me, and the fantastic boneless wings that were sitting in front of me. The wings had an Asian flare of some sort. My beer was still ice cold. I was at my local Neighborhood Applebee's. Not one of my regular spots, but there I was sitting by myself, minding my own business after a long day of work. The fella next to me, I don't recall his name, struck up a conversation. He was in his late 40's, with dark hair, heavy set frame, and a friendly face. I don't remember how he started the conversation, but as hard as I tried to avoid it, we started talking.

It seems I often get sucked into some deep conversations that I would rather avoid. This is typically the case, as I would much rather sit in silence after the many shared words with students all day. I am not unfriendly; I just feel a person only has so many words they can speak in one day. And some people should only be allowed to say so many words in one day. As a special education teacher, I feel like I speak way too much while at work.

Nevertheless, I found myself in another deep conversation. I remember that this stranger said he was waiting for his daughter to get out of some intense counseling down the street. He was very forth coming in our conversation. This may be a superpower that I have developed from my job, because strangers often tell me some deep stuff. I am talking about people I have just met, telling me about things my own family and I do not talk about. The things he and his daughter were going through sounded very similar to the type of teaching I was doing at the time, so it continued our chat.

Our conversation led to me telling him that I was a special education teacher. He responded, with a laugh, and said, "I am a recovering teacher." I laughed a little, and out of curiosity I asked him, "What does that mean?" He told me he had taught for several years, but as his family grew and life expenses increased, he simply could not financially afford to be a teacher. He had two daughters, a wife, a mortgage, counseling costs, and all of life's other expenses to pay for. This stranger told me how much he had loved teaching, but simply could not financially afford to continue the career path. He went into some type of business I can't recall.

It was at this point in the conversation that anything else he said, I have forgotten. I was already up in my head, thinking about those two words. His story, along with his struggle, was completely different than mine, but something was there. The causes and effects of what he had said were, also, only mildly related to mine. But still... It was the simple two words that he uttered, recovering teacher, that started this wheel in my head.

His words led me down a weird, windy path of confusing and intriguing thoughts. Those two words followed me into the woods. I was in my late 20's and had already been teaching for about 6 years when this enlightening moment presented itself. I had made it past the 5-year mark that many teachers do not.

According to Fabiola Cineas, in an article put out Aug 18, 2022, "...beginning teachers have among the highest rates of turnover of any group of teachers. Overall, more than 44 percent of new teachers leave the profession within five years." On top of this high attrition rate, I was working with the most "impossible" of students. To give a clearer perspective of where this teacher comes from, the following is a short summary about my early career as a teacher. We will dive a bit deeper into the specifics of my career throughout the book and especially in Chapter 5, Why My Perspective Matters.

In many jobs, if you worked for multiple companies (in this case schools) and switched from year to year, it would mean some type of failure or weird circumstances. Moving from one job to another has never really been a highlight of any resume or a good quality to brag about. Constant movement could show low commitment or some type of complications within the individual from year to year. Constantly moving jobs could mean many things; mostly hard, complicated and negative type things. Not in this case.

My story has similar migration patterns, but for different reasons. The school I grew up in, my first school as a teacher, was a private placement for special education students. We provided a type of education that multiple districts simply could not. Districts did not have the trained staff or the resources to help these students. In the district setting, these students could not safely or effectively be taught. Our education was, first and foremost, based on behavior. Districts sent the students to us until their behavior was improved enough for them to return to their campus. Often, students could not return. It was emotionally and sometimes physically draining.

As our school grew, we supported many districts around the metropolitan area of Phoenix, AZ. Then, as now, I strived to be the best teacher on campus. I am just too damn competitive. (Oh yeah, this book is most certainly for you teachers who are way too competitive in life and accidentally brought that into the teaching realm) I was good enough to be promoted within the company and used for my strong work ethic quickly. With continued success, our school then provided satellite programs within the district schools as a transition step for the students back into their homeschool. I went to many of these schools and experienced a tremendous amount.

This unique introduction into the education world is an important piece to why this book has been written. Without this nomadic introduction to education, I would never have seen so much. I might have missed out on all the similar patterns from one school to the next. I may have very different views without those colorful early experiences in my career. *To be very direct and connect some dots for later, I may not have been able to identify these patterns if I was so committed (so damn stuck)*

to the same school environment as most teachers.

I worked with many districts in those first 5-7 years and had seen too much. I noticed many differences along the way, including poverty level, cultures, and ethnic backgrounds. These separations existed among staff, students, and families. I saw different leadership styles, disciplinary models, dress codes. I saw good and bad decisions, legal and illegal actions, along with much, much more. Still, no matter where I ended up each year, there was always an echoing pattern. I didn't recognize it at the time. Only because of the Applebee's interaction, combined with some important time away in the woods, something was coming to light in my 7th or 8th year of teaching. An undeniable pattern was starting to present itself, no matter where I was teaching. I hadn't figured out what it was at this point. Not even close. I only knew I didn't want any part of it.

After I met the Applebee's guru, I couldn't stop thinking about what this "recovering teacher" comment meant for me. Did I need to skip having a family so I could afford to live off the salary of a teacher? Was I bound to be living paycheck to paycheck for the rest of my career? Did I need to meet a sugar mama to enjoy all the splendors of life's lap of luxury? Oh boy, did I try. LOL Or was I just holding on, waiting for another career if I wanted more in life, just like the Applebee's man? Had I wasted my time, effort, and money in college? I simply could not stop thinking about when and how I would need to recover from teaching.

At that time, recovering teacher meant that I had an illness. If I remained a teacher, I would be sick. The longer I remained a teacher, the sicker I could become. As a special education teacher, trying to be the best, I apparently was extra sick. Would there ever be an anecdote? Even though I questioned it almost every day, I continued to be the best teacher I possibly could. I felt successful at work. I felt like I was better than others at work, because of my great efforts and sacrifices. I continued to try to do everything I was asked to do, even if I had to do it after work and over the weekends. I climbed and climbed that ladder, no matter how hard. I even went back to school myself, to become a master in my field. I went back to school to get my master's in special education at night, while working what statistics call the improbable, impossible job!

There is a chance I was not only unwell as a teacher, but also unknowingly killing myself. According to Frontline Education, an article put out by Annie Buttner, Contributing Consultant, on 8/4/2021, "special education teachers have a turnover rate, nearly twice that of general education teachers, at 12.3%." As mentioned, I had already beaten the statistics. I had doubled the time that was expected, and I was making decent money. I started to think that the man, the guru of Applebee's, simply wasn't cut out to be a teacher; he was not as strong as I was. The hard-working, unbeatable, competitive side of me told me to keep going.

I unknowingly was developing a type of biased art. I painted a picture that made me look really good in the middle. If I looked at school and neglected the rest of my life, I would be on top of the world. I was the best! I was successful, while he was not. He did not have the charisma that I did. That ex-teacher, like so many others, did not have the special that I brought into special education. Applebee's man must have been lacking. I had seen all those teachers come and go in those younger years of teaching. They were all weak, just like the Applebee's man. I remained strong! The longer I remained teaching, I could call myself persistent, unwavering, and confident, etc. I was just better than the rest, I could tell myself. Those that could not endure teaching were weak in my mind.

"Not everyone can be a teacher." "You must be so patient." "Thank you for your service", from a stranger... These are just a few things folks say to you when they find out you are an educator. I could continue to call myself all those things as long as I kept going. There is no doubt in my mind these kinds of comments make all teachers feel good. It made me feel great at the beginning of my career. It could almost make a person feel super important and special because of their job. It may even spark the ear of the person, in that profession, every election year...LOL My artistic, biased, outlandish, overall selfish view of myself made me think that maybe I was already a recovered teacher. It also

carried me through year to year, well, until it didn't.

Chapter 2 - Just the Way it is

I remember when I started to tell my friends that I didn't really feel like going out. They joked and told me I was getting old, but I meant and felt it. I started to tell my family I couldn't show up for the BBQ and felt their disappointment. Yet, I still didn't go. I didn't have enough energy to go to the gym or if I did show up my workouts were lacking. I ate out at restaurants way more than I needed to, as a 30-year-old man at the time. I know how to cook; I just didn't want to.

I didn't want to do a lot of things after work, all the while becoming more satisfied with doing nothing. I didn't know or realize how important it was at the time, but I was draining myself at work. I put so much effort into my job that I was losing my energy to do the rest of my life. Besides neglecting family, not hanging out with friends, skipping my work outs, I stopped doing my hobbies. I stopped doing so many of the things in life that might matter most.

This is the same that many people do in their professional lives, not just teachers. Beyond just the actual physical work, we spend so much of our effort, patience, energy, etc. that we just don't have enough left for when we get home. Like a small leak, without any realization, we stop doing our outside of school tasks, chores, and fun with the same passion. Sometimes the leak is so small we don't ever notice. We still do the things we love, but it is lacking in one way or another. Or, like most, we give our hobbies of the past up, because we no longer have the time, or no longer make the time. Some of us make up excuses like we are getting old, but really, we stopped working out years ago and that's why we are "old."

Simply said, it is hard to find balance sometimes between work and the rest of life. Most people weigh much more heavily on the job side of things. We try to please work expectations before life for some reason. Oh yeah, money. I guess we all do need some of that. *We invest so much time and effort into our careers earning money that we misspend; we then have little energy left for the truest of investments.* I started to feel this imbalance early in my career, so I started looking for advice as I had some great friends and incredible mentors in my life.

I told my boss that schoolwork was killing my motivation to work out after the school day. He was a big dude and so were many of my co-workers. At that time, my job included physical management. We had to physically manage high school students who became upset and physically aggressive. I am not a big dude, but I still wanted to be the best. Old habits are hard to break. I needed to work out for my job and, on top of that, for my own mental and physical health. My boss told me to work out at 4:30 in the morning, before work like he did. He explained that was the only way, because he also didn't have the energy after work. He said there was no way for him to know when he would be done with work each evening, so it was just easier that way. He had adjusted his whole life schedule to make sure he could still workout, all based on work. I told him that was crazy. I needed my beauty sleep and such. "That's just the way it is," he told me.

Throughout the years I worked with some great people. These hard-working people challenged my own work ethic and made me a better person for the time we spent together. I am super grateful to these folks over the years. Most often these talented coworkers moved on to bigger "better" places. Many of them moved away from teaching completely. On the other end of the spectrum of workers, I worked with some very incompetent, lazy, excuse making folks that could drive a hard-working person crazy. This book is not meant for these types of folks either. I want to stress that there are many teachers out there that still need to learn a work ethic, before they try to balance it. I know there are some very shitty teachers out there! I have worked with them year after year. This probably contributes to the good ones leaving. More accurately, it most certainly adds to the stress and workload that causes good teachers to leave their jobs. When I approached my leaders at the time, my boss, and friends about working with people like this, those damn words kept coming. "That's just the way that it is."

I will let you know you here, I am not ignorant about this area. My stupidity is under control... In other words, I know there are reasons that certain positions attract specific demographics. Many of these positions in schools pay so little and often are very hard to fill. In many cases, just having a body in the seat is success now a days. That includes teachers, sadly. It really doesn't matter, even if she knits in the classroom at the back of the room, has early onset dementia, and a 5th grade student is asked to keep an eye on her for health reasons. Even if we can't find him anywhere when we need him. Even if they only show up when they want. Even if... even if. None of those an exaggeration. These are all real scenarios that played out because there simply are not enough people to fill the needed roles of teaching. This leads to some interesting characters filling these most important roles. "That is just the way it is."

Here we must talk about Mr. M. He couldn't knit, he was of sound mind, but still he was the Webster Dictionary definition of a lacking employee. Mr. M was a great guy. He was articulate, friendly, and computer smart. I called upon him often to help me with computer stuff, as I am not computer smart. He was a terrible teacher though. As a team member he was lacking. This guy was so busy doing nothing, nowhere always. I heard the question, "Where is Mr. M?", so many times that it stood out as one of those damn patterns. This guy was so great at avoiding his work that he couldn't be caught. We couldn't fire him because we couldn't find him to tell him. LOL Not really, of course. We just couldn't hire anyone else. If we did fire and rehire, there was always the chance that the next person could be worse. "That's just the way it is."

I am also aware of the many other factors that lead to people struggling at work. There are so many more important reasons outside of the job that influence a person's work performance. People have families to think about, care for, and love. People have friends, hobbies, and life to distract them from being good workers. And most important for many now a days, people have pets to feed, walk, love and take better care of than they do themselves. Regular people have a lot of things that pull from being a great employee.

I had a problem! I could not, would not stand for this. At the time, I did not recognize the importance of the other side. Moreover, I created a pattern for myself that led me to avoid it. At the time, I was nowhere close to a recovering teacher. It seemed so simple to me. We needed to hire people who were willing to work hard. We needed to fire those who did not work hard. Others needed to pick up their work ethic and WE could "save the world." I couldn't do it by myself... If others worked as hard as I did, I wouldn't come home so exhausted. If my team would just be like me, we could do it. My passion was as strong as my ignorance!

Some of my coworkers hated me for working so hard. Looking back, I must agree with them. I brought unneeded stress into the workplace trying to do too much. I took work much too seriously sometimes. A good friend tried to help me through these feelings at the time. Somewhere in his peptalk with me, he said, "You need to bend before you break." Another way of saying, "that's just the way it is." He was right of course. There are some things you just can't change. There will always be a Mr. M., or a prehistoric knitter of yarn on the team. In these cases, teachers like me need to change how they deal with it. That was the truest "Just the way it is" for me. I was the problem!

I have always wanted to be the best at what I am doing. That is just the way it is with me. I am much too competitive sometimes. It has put strain on some relationships and stress in unneeded places in my life. My competitive nature has made my team members feel inferior or less valued sometimes. On the other hand, there are quite a few benefits to this mentality. College degrees, soccer championships, bull riding buckles, and some super cool antlers to name a few. I work hard at almost everything I do. This usually leads to good results, especially with the things I am passionate about! Of course, like anyone, there are many things I neglect and am just not good at. I have never tried to be the best at geometry, typing, or chess. I am terrible at those things. I don't enjoy those things either. But, when I want to be good at something, I work my ass off to be the best.

Working in a school with this mentality can be a dangerous thing. If never noticed and purposefully managed, it is the hardest working teachers that burn out. See, it turns out that working hard as a teacher doesn't mean you get to finish early or even get to take a break. Working hard as a teacher is counter intuitive, like a catch 22. The harder you work as a teacher; the more students feel how much you care for them. Suddenly you become one of the favorite teachers and students come to you more and more often. They will come to you at lunch and during your prep. If you miss school for a day, they put up posters for you around the neighborhood like you're a lost puppy.

As you gain the trust of students, they release their deepest secrets and passions for life. Students tell you about their relationship issues, fears, family drama, and so much more. They share the latest on anything and everything with the teachers who will make the time to listen. Students open their hearts to teachers who know the significant importance of making time beyond the curriculum.

It is just the same with your coworkers. The harder you work; the more other teachers trust you and know they can lean on you. Struggling teachers will find you specifically to act as their sage. They will lean on you rather than a bad principal, bad special education director, or bad boss. Then, because you are who you are - you say, "What's wrong?" or "Of course you can come in" and "no problem." Over and over, you do this. First week after week, then month to month, and eventually year after year.

In addition, if you continue to be good at your job, the powers that exist will give you more and more work. You will be noticed for your efforts, then complimented, maybe rewarded – followed by another responsibility. Administration will give you more work until you are not good at your job. Any good boss/business is trained for this. Good, competitive teachers, like you and me, must understand when to say no. This is especially true currently, with teacher shortages everywhere. It is okay to say no to the never-ending extra responsibilities that can be added to your plate from above. Hard workers in a school will always be overworked and undercompensated in their job place, but especially as teachers. And that is another just the way it is.

We have all heard students, teachers, parents, and everyone else involved with teaching talk about the 'what' we are teaching. Since I was a child, complaining about what is being taught in the classroom has been an evident pattern. I know I did as a student and still do as a teacher. I don't want to get into the historical, religious, political, and financial reasons that go into 'what' we teach. I just want to point out some evident patterns that may have been overlooked.

Students complain, "Why do I have to learn this? I am never going to use it anyway." Parents can easily point out that they literally do not ever use much of the 'what' they learned in the classrooms of their youth. The few parents who still help their children do homework look the stuff up on Google, YouTube, or call their "smartest friend" to get the answers. I have seen teachers look up on Google the very information they are experts of. The teacher experts, me included, look up some of the information that is supposedly the most important thing to educating this youth. Most adults might agree that many jobs do not use a lot of the information taught in schools. The only job who uses some of that information is the damn teacher and they don't even know it half the time.

It's almost as if some of 'what' we teach is a mirage. It is made to look so beautiful and rewarding and it leads to nowhere. It leads to a degree, of course. Having a degree is better than not. Having your doctorate is higher than having your master's is higher than... Stupid ladder!

I learned only so much about teaching while paying ASU all that money. I often got even less sitting in a room with other adults, "learning" new strategies I rarely could use. I wasted so much time participating in staff developments to learn recycled, updated, renamed bullshit from past years. The truth is, I learned much more about how to be a good teacher, well after graduation. The best teaching I have ever done was far off that ladder.

I learned how to be a good teacher, driving a student and his grandmother to get haircuts after work. I became a better teacher when I showed up for some of my students' athletic events on the weekends. Delivering holiday dinners made me a better teacher and so much more. The best parts of life are learned outside of most of that silly curriculum.

It's almost like we just fill the time of both children and adults with anything to keep them from thinking differently. *We never really use a lot of what we teach for anything, except to hold over someone who does not know it.* This is the way it has been since I was a kid in the classroom until now as a veteran teacher. If that does not qualify for another 'just the way it is', then I do not know how to uncover your eyes.

Again, I am only half an idiot. Much of the early curriculum is incredibly important in creating a functioning, educated, active citizen. I realize there is much in the curriculum that does matter, even if we do forget it down the line. I realize that the simple act of learning is so important; I am a teacher. I could go into the science of synapsis, brain growth, etc. I could continue by stressing the incredible importance of social learning in school, in addition, to what it does for young men and women to stay away from gang violence and drug use. We could also include that there is simply not much else to do with the ever-growing population of children, after the urbanization of the 19th century. There is such incredible importance to the institution of a school, in addition to what the students learn. I am not saying school is a waste of time. *I am saying there is a whole lot of wasted time in school.*

For example, the curriculum in many places makes students learn levels of math that truly are never used again. It often makes them learn a level of math they are not ready for, creating large gaps in students' learning. In Arizona, I have watched so many schools push students through year after year. This puts teachers and so many students into a backwards battle before the school year even begins. Why intentionally plan for such a struggle? Math could be the most specialized class of all, but no, we just push students through from one level to the next. Math could easily focus on the level of a student, along with a specific need directed towards a future job. Math could focus on teaching the students real life skills. But for some reason students need to know what time 2 different trains will meet in Chicago. Oh wait, that one adds up to some useful thinking... You know what I mean. Well beyond my world of special education, many general education students are sitting in a classroom with not enough prior knowledge to connect to what is being taught on the board. Students are taught to memorize equations to find parts of shapes they will never see in the real world and then grow up with so little money sense, or function behind what they can do with numbers. Math may be the most important class that should not move on without mastery or close to it. What is the point? Is that just the way it is?!

A different example of wasted school time is in History class. As a lover of learning History early in my life, I couldn't see this one until I really got out of my patterns and took a good look at my own historical past. It seems to me we teach history that is wrong and then reteach it at higher levels to debate whether it is right or wrong. No doubt there are some inspiring moments and great figures of the past. Some of those stories teach morals and values, which is great. And, of course, learning our *biased* American history makes us better functioning, educated, active citizens...

Or does it? There is so much round about wasted time in learning History when you take a step back. "But history teaches us, and we learn from our mistakes", they say. Is that why they also say, "history repeats itself?"

Come on, unless you have your own family history down and a timeline set for your own future, learning other people's history is a huge waste of time. Until you have the essentials of life, which many kids do not, history as an essential part of the curriculum is incredibly wasteful. No wonder so many students think the subject to be boring.

Even in saying this, I still love learning certain parts of History. I still teach History for goodness' sake... I even still waste some time at night falling asleep to a documentary on television. That is my choice as an adult, who almost has it together. I have almost figured out my past and my future. Well, at least now I am trying. Students could be taught much more important things than a lot of what is in the History curriculum. Just the way it is.

We then teach sciences that reach far into the heavens and well into the depths of the earth to students who have one parent, barely enough food, a sick little brother at home, and so little hope or understanding for their future. We make these same students "learn" chemistry equations that 99% will never use again. Guess what. There is a science that can be taught that helps a child that has only one parent at home. In fact, there is science and some morals that could be taught that would help to prevent one parent at home in the first place. There is another science that will allow for personal care and self-esteem to blossom. There are philosophical practices and sciences that will make a student believe in themselves and have confidence in their future. Once they have that down, then start sending them into the heavens. They will make it!

As a special education teacher, I have even more of a different perspective. I have watched so many teachers stress year to year about getting through the curriculum, while I try to teach them things from multiple years of past curriculum. LOL Very rarely does this work to get a student caught up. Most of the time it does not. It usually turns into a bigger problem. It cycles and creates more academic deficiencies. They pile into something even the best of special education teachers cannot repair. Most times, all of those pushed on academic problems turn into a whole other beast. Students with self-esteem issues, anxiety issues, performance issues, and much more.

Most teachers complain about the bunch of attention deprived youths doing anything and everything to get a laugh. Even worse, there is a growing group of young people who have already given up on life. Too many students just don't care. These students don't just not care about school. They don't care about anything, except some made up, entertaining, bull shit on their phone. Even good teachers get caught up on every one of the behavior problems that keep us from teaching all that lavender scented bull shit mentioned above. I used to.

I used to believe I could change how students behave. I spent too much energy believing I was an important piece of the puzzle that made it all work. If one is not careful, they may become more of the problematic cycle, wasting their own time within that system. There is another way.

On top of 'what' we teach, teachers point out year after year that there is not enough time to teach all that is expected. If the curriculum is so important, why do teachers cruise through the standards with very little mastery on the way. Then we reach down so deep, multiple grade levels, to try and raise a kid up year after year. Educators are expected to teach the curriculum propaganda by a certain date, no matter the integrity of the student's knowledge. What the hell for?

Failing students are then passed on from year to year, without knowing the building blocks for learning at the next grade level. Some loving teachers even lie to themselves, to give their students passing grades. I have found myself many times bending the rules out of love. Some kind of gray zone I created in the curriculum. I think many use this gray zone of teaching to help their students get through.

If what we are teaching year to year is so important, why do we push kids through without mastery? Why do we push problems through to the next teacher, year after year. It's almost as if what we teach really doesn't matter! Okay, not almost. It doesn't matter as much as some teachers try to make it matter. Stop doing it to yourself! Stop pretending that your curriculum is so damn important!

If my words still are not reaching you, maybe the gorilla from Daniel Quinn's book, My Ishamel, will better speak your language. If you have never read the book and you need someone more esteemed than a lowly special education teacher to teach you, give it a shot. His chapter, titled School Daze, may just help you understand more clearly. To sum up the chapter with just one quote from this articulate gorilla; "It's got to look like something r-e-e-e-a-l-l-y useful." The key word in there is look. Much of what we teach is far from useful...

I am going to skip over some of the politics behind this decision making, but again, it is not out of a lack of information. The gorilla told me everything I need to know... LOL On top of that, there are a whole lot of contradicting theories, statistics, opinions, etc. to complicate things. There is too much information; we confuse acquiring this information with knowledge. All this creates is a tangle of angry, confused, disappointed, greedy people arguing in no direction. It is not worth the time of a recovering teacher. I am skipping over these things to keep you on point. *I am ignoring these complications the way a recovering teacher needs to.*

If a building was built to the same standards as teaching, it would not last. It would not be built. OSHA would shut that shit down. You simply could not build without a strong foundation. This is what school systems are asking us to do as teachers. Build better children, though you must start with less parts, so little time, numerous distractions, then fewer and fewer employees. This is the school system that keeps us good teachers looking and caring in the wrong direction, focused on some of the least important things in life. That's just the way it is.

Out of some resent and anger, I saved this one for last. Though later in the book, you may see this point can be the most important just the way it is. It was for me. Years in to climbing the ladder of my teaching career, my least favorite principal bragged about how many schools she worked for, while I explained the hardships that her policies were putting on our program.

I had run the self-contained special education classroom for the school, 5th-8th grade, successfully for 2 years before she was **given** the principalship. I had left my first teaching job to work at this location; it was a big deal for me. I had made it into that cushy district, the one with the good retirement. I ran the rat race, then climbed the ladder. I was still climbing the ladder at that point in my career.

This leader of our school was new to the position; she was a puppet. She had replaced the non-puppet type. She took over for the confident, hard-working principal, that was a big part of the reason why I had decided to work at that district/school in the first place. As the puppet and I were talking about her disciplinary lacking and her inability to provide my classroom with the legal requirement of staff, she said, "Special Education has always been this way in the schools I have worked. That's just the way it is." She used the exact words I later used to name this chapter… Bless her for that.

And screw that! This is not the way it should be and would not be the way for me. I did not return to that district I had worked so hard to get to. I jumped right off the very ladder that got me to the top, and since, I have been using it for campfires in the woods.

After working as a teacher for over a decade, I quit! I was scared to death, but felt so incredibly free in some weird way. I had the whole summer to see what would happen.

It was during this confusing transition of my life that I started to think about writing this book. It then took me 3 years to get at it. Just another example of everything I had not yet learned to put into practice; something I am still working on. I was so busy at work, I took forever to just start typing something different than lesson plans, emails to parents, and IEP paperwork. It was about this time that the meaning of recovering teacher was starting to evolve into something I could share with my colleagues too. This book is for teachers who want to be their own kind of teacher, instead of just the way it is.

Chapter 3 — Wasted Will Power

I read a book once to help me with some increasing anxiety and work ethic that was lacking in my favorite hobby of the time, bull riding. My experience with riding bulls has proven to be incredibly important as I walk down life's path. It's a huge part of why I think my perspective is a bit different than most other teachers too. The sport and folks associated with it, along with some words in the book I read, were an equation that added up for me. The book and the science behind my thoughts come from Roy Baumeister, then explained by Amy L. Baltzell in her book, Living in the Sweet Spot. Baltzell speaks about will power, according to Baumeister, and puts her own perspective on it in the sport training world.

My simple mind thought of it as this; willpower is within all of us like a filled vessel. As we use our willpower throughout the day, that cup empties. Simple, right? I used to think of willpower as the *ability to not do something*. I used to think a person needs the will power to *not* have another cookie. For me, to *not* have a chocolate shake every night. I thought people practice the will power to *not* hit that annoying person in the face or flip that guy off in traffic. It turns out, will power is much more than what we don't do. Will power is also the things we choose to do. It is right there in the name. I am not sure why I viewed willpower in such a negative way, but it turns out, willpower is the will to do something and the will not to. Both what we do and what we don't do add up to how much willpower we use throughout the day. *All* the choices we make during the day fill and empty our willpower cups.

Imagine a diet that you have followed perfectly. You spend weeks on end with no sugar, no fat, no carbs, no whatever. You walk tall, full of willpower, right past that ice cream aisle without regret. You go without beer for 123 days in a row. We put so much effort into our diets, but at a certain point the craving just takes over and we lose that will power. For some, this battle happens minute by minute, hour by hour, or daily; for others, they can last longer.

But these dietary battles do not happen alone. Our food choices are under constant attack as they interact with all the other mysteries of the day. Every little decision drains our cup, sometimes with no realization. Other times, we can really feel the strain of making that decision, like me ordering food at any new restaurant. It is all a short-term verse long-term balance of the all-inclusive willpower, when you really pay attention to it.

Think about that routine that you have fought to create or change, and somewhat accomplished, that just falls through one day. How about when we hold our tongue as long as we can, just to spill our guts? What about that habit that we are trying to fight off? Right when we're not looking, it comes from out of nowhere with a sucker punch. We all lose that fight with willpower here and there. Is there a chance our tiny little decision making earlier in the day added up to that? Isn't it usually a stressful day or some type of bad event that causes us to justify our loss of willpower?

What most of us may not recognize is how this willpower principle works on a micro scale verse the macro scale and then how it all ties together. I didn't realize until I truly broke away from my patterns, lost with my thoughts in the woods. We are so caught up in our day-to-day jobs, traffic, and other decision-making responsibilities, we fail to see what is right in front of us. There are so many tiny choices we make throughout the day that we may not realize the powerful effects they add up to. All these small decisions have a major influence on the overall amount of our willpower and then how we use it. Most of us give so much willpower to our jobs, by the end of the day we fail to do the things we really want in life. We do so much to please others and accomplish work tasks, we forget to save some for ourselves.

Some of us constantly think we want to learn to cook, workout, eat healthier, save money, etc., but by the end of the day we have spent so much of our willpower on work that we have too little left to fully accomplish these goals. Hell, for many of us, we spend so much of our willpower just to get up on time for work. Then we use some more on the drive to work without fighting the person who cut us off in traffic. We continue to spill our willpower each morning we open our new list of emails, without throwing the computer against the wall. By 9:00 one person needs a cigarette, one needs a second energy drink, another needs to see the school counselor, while one is eating the exact food they swore they wouldn't eat the night before. All the small, miniscule choices we make add up to the big choices we make or don't make, and all of it is a delicate balance of emptying and filling our willpower cup. Now think of this from a teacher's perspective.

As a teacher, we use so much willpower patiently talking to our students; we explain the same thing so many times. We repeat instructions, rules, and that one student's name at least 3o times every single day. It could drive a person crazy. Then, we teachers deal with ridiculous demands from "superiors" that know so little. This might be the biggest misuse of willpower, listening to people who truly know nothing about what they speak of. We then cover classes because that same Ms. Soandso has an "emergency" again or the district pissed off/let down the substitute teacher service. We do all this while we hold our bowel movements, for goodness' sake.

Most teachers even bring their work home with them daily, both figuratively and literally. Have you seen the teacher's wheely suitcases? Some teachers have whole wagons with walls and levels. It's absurd. I was going through Teacher College when those silly suitcases became so popular for teachers to use. It almost made me regret becoming a teacher back then. In that instance, I swore to never drag a basket full of stress with me anywhere. We teachers do too much, spending so much of our willpower at work. Then we literally drag it home with us to ensure that we have even less time left for our family, friends, and personal goals at the end of the day. Wasted wheel power if you ask me. LOL

I will admit that I just don't answer the phone sometimes, because I don't have enough patience left to hear what my sister's problems are at the end of the day. When I took the time, I noticed I skipped a lot of phone calls over the years, even from family and friends. You know damn well I answered my classroom phone when the principal called. I've snapped on my own mother because she forgot what I told her a week ago, but I will repeat myself over and over **and over** with a smiling face to the students. I have lied to my brother and friends, because I would rather sit alone, do nothing, or pretend to watch a repeat television show. I have often sat at home alone and complained to myself about my own triumphs of the day. As a teacher, it feels like right around 4:30 I need to turn off. I think people call it their social battery now a days. Teachers lose a lot of that battery while at school, especially the burnt-out teachers who don't want to be there. It's impossible not to.

I've made a pattern of treating myself poorly outside the school doors, while acting like an angel, a saint, Buddha himself at school. I used up most of my willpower on the wrong things, **work!** Don't misunderstand me. I love helping my students! I love helping other teachers! I love when Ms. Soandso wears that skirt on Thursdays. LOL I enjoy many things about my job, but there were certain things I was wasting my willpower on, because that was just the way it was as a teacher. And that is what I was becoming as a teacher. I emptied my cup throughout the day for others, without ever thinking to fill it back up for myself. So many good teachers and good people do this.

We all know this is not a problem for some people in the workplace. Some people miss more days than they work. Others crush more candy and clash so many clans when they are there, they don't get any work done. There are a lot of people who seemingly do not know how to focus on work. In my view, there are a growing number of people who just don't have pride in their work anymore. Who cares? Just another made-up stat if I wanted to. I guess I need to stress the point again, this book is not for those of you who have not worked enough to get lost in it. I was proudly, unknowingly lost in work, like I know so many other good teachers are. I was working closer and closer towards burnout year after year. This book is to pull those of us out of thinking that drowning at work is just the way it is and wasting our willpower on it.

It is right around here where some of you will read this and, maybe, start to question the author's attitude or my own burn out status. It is right around here where some of you will give up on the idea because it is against what you have convinced yourselves. It is the same thing that I fight with myself each day, because I/we have been programmed to think in this certain way. It is the whole rat race thing and climbing the ladder. *It's part of the American Dream that no one really warns you about.* I have been tricked, like so many, into thinking that working hard at work is more important than working hard at life. Maybe even a step further, we could be working joyfully rather than hard. This is the most internally controversial part of the book for me as a self-proclaimed hard worker. This has been difficult to admit and to try to change, but hard work is not always a good thing.

Not all teachers are going through what I am, of course. I bet there are teachers out there that have everything figured out. They use classroom calculators to do their taxes, while cooking a five-course meal, and doing laundry at the same time. They even have their ABC magnets spelling something correctly on the fridge at home. Of course, there are teachers out there who have found the balance between work and life. And maybe there are even a few teachers who aren't faking a large part of their day and truly do love their jobs as much as they act. Of course, there are superhuman people that can just keep giving and giving every part of their day without any negative side effects. Let me just stop there. No, there is not!

According to my data collected around the copy machine and those silly national statistics there are not many teachers living a well-balanced life with their career. More teachers than not are unhappy with multiple parts of their jobs. The usual complaints include overcrowded classrooms, behavior of students, ignorant leadership, and of course the wasted time in unneeded staff meetings. In 16 years, I have consistently seen teachers come and go and hear them complain about the same old stuff. It is another way we choose to lose our willpower. It's typical to complain about work, everyone does it. But you don't have to make a pattern of it, and you won't have to as you find recovery.

On the other hand, how about intentionally taking some good feelings home with you? Teachers can sometimes feel so great about work and what they are accomplishing that they take it home with them on purpose. Why not? Some of the things that happen in a day of teaching are miraculous and make a person want to share it with the world. It is, but I still think that is part of the problem that causes the imbalance. I have gone home so excited to talk about work stuff, that I didn't even realize my closest people were going through their own shit. I have made a habit of going home to talk to whoever about work so much that they know my staff and students by name or nicknames.

Go home to your family and start asking about them. After work, go out with your friends and talk about something personal, meaningful, and rewarding rather than wasting your will power bitching or even celebrating work.

How many times do we answer the question, "How was your day?", with a story about work. Almost always. You don't have to though. If you feel you must, go ahead and lean your story in a positive direction. Only share those stories that lift you and those around you. Just not too much... I went through that faze to justify things... it still leads to burnout.

One should not be a bigger mascot for a system/business/school than for one's own family or themselves. Don't find too much identity in your workplace. No matter what colors we put on it, no matter how much you may start to feel like a family, no matter what. You and your coworkers are not family. You shouldn't be. We humans do not have enough willpower to take care of two families and then ourselves. At least I don't.

I have fallen in love with coworkers and still have some love for them to this day. I have made some great friends over the years as a teacher too, but that doesn't mean I have to try to be friends with all of them. It doesn't mean I have to give any attention to some of them, if you know what I am saying... I know I will continue to find friends through work that *feel like family,* and I will love them. That is a part of who I am, like so many empathetic teachers. But they are *not my family*.

I use enough willpower trying to help my older brother with his wild entrepreneurship and my single mother age gracefully. I use much more to make sure I don't miss my little brother too much, as he has moved across the country. All the while, I use more willpower to fight off onset depression, thinking about friends and family members well gone but never forgotten.

Maybe the reason you start to feel like a family at work is because you are neglecting your own family. I am sorry to say it, but someone has to. Maybe you start to feel like a family at work because you spend too much time there. There is a whole lot more outside of work when you give yourself the time and power to experience it. If you intentionally learn how to pay attention and then use your willpower for you, you may feel it. Your family will start to feel it too.

Schools are just a system, a business, a job for people like any other. One should be careful to separate themselves from what they do as a job and what they do in life. Don't spend too much time there and, sure as hell, don't bring it home with you, physically or emotionally. Nevertheless, I am not here to argue a moot point. This book is not meant for folks who just like to argue. Wait, that's me sometimes... dang teachers. LOL.

More specifically, this message will be missed by those who pour their hearts out to the point of emptiness, just to complain about it! It is an easy trap to get set in to. This is one of the worst patterns so many teachers follow. I made up a whole lot of excuses for what I was doing until I decided to change, or until I saw what was really happening to me. This message is for the rest of you who self admittedly know you need to start filling your cup.

Now, those well-aged, life-long, die hard teachers have drained their cups a long time ago. You can see it in their wrinkles. LOL. These poor teachers learned from those before them, without ever thinking there could be something different. It is one of those patterns I almost became. It is a pattern that is incredibly hard to fight and drains too many good teachers. Hard-working teachers are so overwhelmed, lost in the system, stuck *waiting for retirement*, barely living day to day, they couldn't know another way. They lost any version of recovery a long time ago and turned into the hardened, monotone, student-hating teachers we know them for. For some reason, they are usually an English teacher; I am sure it is all the grading they take home with them that has this diminishing effect. Excuse my honesty and directness, but we all know one of them. Whether English teacher or not, they sit silently in the back of the staff meeting, waiting to point out another blunder by the higher ups as soon as the chance presents. Or, after the meeting, they rally with other rattled coworkers and point out how stupid and wasteful the meeting was. They lead the convoy to happy hour and lead the conversation always toward the negative. We call it venting, but really, it's wasted will power. These types of teachers are almost always right, but unknowingly they spread the pattern further. These experienced educators are perfect models for young teachers on how to empty their own cups.

No matter how much willpower has been wasted over the years, it is never too late. It just may be a bit harder to figure yourself out and break those patterns. I was about 10 years in when I started to practice recovery; just a baby compared to some of you old timers. As an experienced veteran teacher, look back on your time and efforts to find the waste. Find what frustrates you the most and stop doing it. Just stop.

See what happens, see who says something, who says nothing, just see. Good, hardworking teachers, I can easily say to you -nothing bad is going to happen. If you dig deep, you can replace your bad habits with something new and refreshing. For you seasoned veterans of teaching it is most important that you find new and refreshing ways to fill your cups. Your cups have been draining for much too long for the wrong reasons.

Younger teachers, on the other hand, put on the front while at school and go home stressed to cry themselves to sleep. Other young guns do anything they need to, hyped up on coffee or energy juice, to get through the gauntlet. Up and coming creatures of habit, following new teacher trends taught in college or whatever their superior asks of them.

I personally bought clothes I couldn't afford to fit in as a young teacher, so I *would look* professional. LOL I went out drinking with colleagues to try and fit in; they always said I was more fun at the bar... Young teachers do so much to impress others; all the while poking holes into our own willpower cups, losing our very selves. A lot of teachers, young and old, even spend their days eating healthily in front of their colleagues and students. At night, they compensate by eating way too much ice cream. Maybe you lean toward the salty snack, a crunchy morsel, or another version of sinful eating late at night. Most of you know exactly what I am talking about. I must point this out. I, along with more teachers than not, try to eat healthier at work than we do at home. We present this image in front of our colleagues and students at work, that is not real. Why? Don't stop eating healthy! But don't eat a certain way for your coworkers to see you. Do it for yourself!

So many teachers, no matter young or old, spend late nights drinking to drown their sorrows of school hardships or to complain about work with their peers. Well, I did at least. I will admit it. And so did most everyone I worked with. We even slowly turned sweet, little, innocent Ms. K into an experienced, shot taking, loud talking, weekly participant. Thursdays are usually the night; it's hard to wait for Friday. I will make up another statistic here. In my experience, well more than half of teachers are drinkers. A good part of them, can and do party like a rock star. Watch out for those educators at the after party! LOL They were at the preparty too.

Just another wasted strategy of dealing with things I have learned. So much fun, so many fun memories, a few of my friends met their wives this way... How can I call this a waste of willpower? Simply, it's a bad habit. Many educators, including myself for a while, are so busy compensating for work at the bar, that we have no idea what we are missing out on. It is another common waste of willpower.

It is no coincidence that the ladder leads in only one direction. Up, to the top. It takes a whole lot of wasted time to get there, and it is a direction I no longer want to put so much focus on. My mom shared a quote with me once, in one of my favorite birthday cards. "Go out on a limb, that's where the fruit is." Once you understand this the way I am practicing, you can start to find recovery as a teacher. It seems teachers think that's just the way it is, all the while wasting their willpower on the wrong things. Just like those that came before them, so many are always trying to get to the top. This book is for anyone who wants to start filling their cup by going out on a limb!

Chapter 4 - 20/20 Vision

Looking back, 2020 was a difficult year for many people in many ways. Our jobs, hobbies, personal lives, and shopping at the damn store were all turned upside down. We were asked to stay inside, wear masks that literally did nothing, stand 6 feet apart, and on and on. I have always been a little oppositional defiant, so this was hard for me. Every aspect of our daily lives made no sense at all, because it was so radically altered. It was all this ridiculousness that allowed me to see more clearly. It was this "difficult time" that brought me to the other side. It wasn't work related at first; it was the dramatic overreaction to the pandemic.

While the rest of the world was freaking out buying toilet paper, I spent an incredibly large amount of time walking and pooping in the woods. LOL While everything was seemingly closed, the woods were wide open. Amid most people doing what they were told and staying indoors, I did the opposite. I never ran out of toilet paper either. And the more I got away, the more my vision began to clear. *We are blinded by the things we see the most.* I just needed to get away to see things differently.

Like most prophets of the past, seclusion was a necessary part of my change. LOL. I don't think I am a prophet, some type of Moses splitting the Red Sea of Education to set the teachers free. I don't, I swear… I just needed to get away from what others were saying and doing. I needed to wash my brain clear of all the patterned bull shit it was filled with. I needed to see the habits I was stuck in before I could even think of changing them.

I included this chapter because it was through these "rough" times of the Covid-19 pandemic that Applebee's man's words started to mean something more to me. So many people were struggling through the made-up stresses during the pandemic, while I was thriving. I was in the woods every weekend, no traffic both ways cause people were scared inside somewhere. I spent the summer traveling, finding a different story than what was on the news. I spent that summer living it up. Not everywhere of course. Many places were closed, but not the ones I wanted to go to. I was finding my own way through the whole made up political mess. I enjoyed what most of the world was complaining about. *Maybe I could do the same thing in my career. Maybe I could enjoy, or at least not waste, what so many teachers seem to hate.* Recovering teacher, once again, was looking a little clearer to me.

The stipulations and changes implemented in 2020, because of the global pandemic, had equally huge impacts on schools. Obviously. Anyone with a teacher friend or a teacher in their family has heard of these Wild West days in teaching. Students had a whole new virtual world in which they could no longer flip off traffic from the bus, run in the halls, vape in the bathroom, plan a fight at the flagpole, etc. Students had a whole new platform to do those things that kids do; boy did they get creative and weird.

I had students go back to bed right in the middle of class. This student changed into his pajamas (did not get naked thankfully), pointed the camera at himself and was asleep within minutes. Students learned about the computer system much more quickly than me and could totally take over a conference. They took over the conference, drew stick figure porn on the virtual white board, etc. I heard of students taking the computer into their dad on the toilet to help them with the audio. Some students were so incredibly lost in their education - that those months, year, and years for some will always be used as an excuse for their learning level.

My behavioral students had such bravery and creativity to do whatever came to mind, because they simply had no meaningful consequences and so little connection with their learning. All in all, most students, no matter how hard a teacher tried, lost something during those times.

From the teacher's side, it was all brand new to most of us too. Many of us were making it up as we went. Some teachers had been teaching in this virtual world before, but for the rest of us it was a whole new beast. I made up some of the weirdest ways to try and engage students in their learning. The hook, some of us call it. Good teachers use some student prior knowledge and some kind of fun to connect students to their lessons when possible. As a special education teacher, for multiple grade levels in a self-contained setting, we lost all the ability to do these most critical steps of learning. They had freedoms they were not ready to have. Students had their pets literally in their laps, a television playing in the background and their phone or food in hand always. Usually chips. In most cases, there were no parents at home to try to help. In other cases, there were parents eavesdropping in the background and watching this shit show. It was sometimes super uncomfortable and embarrassing. It was nearly impossible to try and get students to WANT to learn.

On top of this, the administration was making up even more bullshit than regular; at least in the school I was working in and throughout that district. They handed down the same expectations without any understanding of what it was really like. They informed us of all the legal requirements we had to follow to appease the state, the district, the school board, and the parents. These puppets at the top just passed down everything they were told, no matter how impossible and unreasonable it was. I am sure there were some great leaders out there in the educational world at the time. They were not at my school.

Our school district was one of the last to go to virtual learning, with much controversy over how special education services would be implemented. We had many extra meetings to decide that... We were the first to be made to return shortly later. I couldn't believe what was being made to be so important, with so little regard for some teachers in certain positions. So much wasted will power. And silly me, I was right there wasting it with them.

Teaching through 2020 was forming an incredible gap between students and teachers, just as much as the gap between me and my administration. As terrible as this was looking back, it was this time that really brought light to the same old problems. *No matter the circumstances, the school system is set up to overwork and abuse hard working teachers.* It took the middle of a global pandemic for me to realize this. The pattern was so deep it couldn't be stopped. And at the time I lacked the word no in my vocabulary, at least toward administration.

My cup was constantly leaking. No matter how difficult, we tried, and we "persevered". Shortly after we got the hang of things, our district decided special education students needed to receive services in person. I finally had figured out how to keep a little willpower for myself and more administrative, bureaucratic tape sliced another hole right into the bottom of my cup. As the rest of the world could not go on, some of us teachers had to. Restaurants, parks, gyms, almost everything was closed. However, our school district decided to open their doors for special education students. Like I said, I didn't know how to say no. Other teachers in our district refused, using valid excuses that I didn't have. Self-assured mothers and fathers stayed at home because their kids' schools were closed. Valid. My teaching assistant stayed at home because he feared getting sick and then couldn't figure out how to log in and help from home, all the while getting paid. Not valid. Not fair. There were all kinds of excuses used by teachers. I was unstoppable, unwavering and still thought my extra hard work made me special. So, if the puppet strings said so, I continued the dance. I complained the whole time and pointed out the issues daily to my superiors, but I still thought I was special for being there.

Parents, of course, had the choice to keep their child at home while our school opened, which about 25% of them did. This meant that lessons needed to be provided in person and online, literally double the work. This didn't mean that our school would be fully staffed or supported as some of us teachers and students were thrust back into things. In my school, in the self-contained environment, we had more than half the students in person and the others online. As mentioned, we had only 2 out of 3 of the staff that we should have had working in person. Lucky for me, the other teaching assistant in my room was a big hearted, too giving, hardworking hell of a lady. Unlucky for us, our 3rd team member was, well, just not there.

I included these examples from 2020 just as a mini sample of how schools work year by year. Over worked teachers will always be a huge part of the equation in school systems. I don't think this can be changed. These hard-working teachers need to find a healthy way through it, rather than trying to change it or fight it.

Hindsight is 2020, works well for some word play here. Looking back to 2020, I was trying to fight the system or change it. I was trying to make a point. I focused and pointed out so much negativity to my superiors to prove a point, I was becoming negative. I was a big part of the problem, no matter how hard I worked or how many students "loved" me. I was still naïve, even after my enlightening hikes. I was learning not to waste willpower in a few areas, but not in the most important area for me. We all have our own self-inflicted wounds, when we will admit it.

Above all that I did for my staff, students, and families, I fought the shit that rolls downhill from an unstoppable source. I was trying to fight the system. *This early misunderstanding of fighting "that's just the way it is" was counter intuitive with trying not to waste so much of my will power at work.* I can see clearly now; back in 2020 I was missing a very important piece to recovering teacher. I was missing something that the Applebee's man said nothing about, probably knew nothing about. It was something as clear as day but still hidden in repetition. It was right there in all those patterns that I had seen over the years.

This was the same time when I realized I really wanted to write this. The book needed to be written for me to learn how to recover and for anyone who was willing to listen. Teachers complained in the break room, in the halls, at happy hour. I was right there with them in my own way. Teachers had so much to say, and it was always repeating the same pattern. Still, nothing changed except the faces of the teachers quitting year after year. This made me want to write this book even more. If other teachers were not going to do something about it, I was. Teachers seem to think this is "just the way it is" and the way it will always be. Teachers learn to accept it and applaud themselves for their wasted hard work or they quit the career all together. We teachers often seem to put ourselves on an underground pedestal, as if it's okay. This book is written to inform and re-inform, to emphasize, it is not okay. There is a different way to get through a teaching career, without losing your vision of life.

Chapter 5 – Teaching Perspectives

There is this funny thing I have noticed about us Americans, another pattern. If someone from another country, with a great accent, sometimes a beard, but mostly the accent, says something - we are more prone to believe it. The exact same words, uttered by an average American, just doesn't have the same effect for some reason. The Indian English accent does it for me; I will readily listen to some eastern words of wisdom well before Mrs. Smith from 6th grade English class. I don't understand it really. The same message from a brother, or sister, or parent is more readily rejected, but we listen to these great ideas spoken from an exotic perspective and agree. It seems we hear truth in the message only through another dialect. Then we put down our phones/Instagram/Facebook/etc. and go live such opposite lives as the message we gave another thumbs up. It is a funny thing I first noticed in myself and then in so many others.

If not the accent, there are still other patterns too easily followed. An actor, acting and quoting something written by someone else, is heard well before our closest friends' words of wisdom. I could listen to Morgan Freeman quote things all day long. Some good-looking, great speakers, with a million followers, will be heard for sure. Over and over and over. My sister will send me a great media message, but because she sent it, I lose sight of the message. I am sure my brother has told me some of the best advice that I just don't hear, because he is my brother. Why do so many of us listen to complete strangers' advice? Why don't we listen to the people that know us the best? Not that we always should, but something to pay attention to, I think. I don't know that this is an American pattern alone, but I know it is another pattern I have decided to fight off.

I am happy and blessed to be born in America. I know this. I am grateful, so when you read this don't tell me to move to another country. Don't get mad right away and shut down either. Try to listen a little before your rebuttal. Try to be a little less American for a second. LOL.

Growing up in America, the way I have, has created some serious ill patterns in my life. There were many ingrained habits I had to learn to replace to become a recovering teacher. There is a chance that we Americans are spoiled rotten. I don't know how to explain it completely; it's more of a feeling. I feel it most when I find myself complaining about ridiculous social drama type stuff or hear people arguing about a fictional television show. As a self-proclaimed spoiled American, I decided to investigate it and learn how to replace some of the things I didn't like in myself. I am still learning to replace a bunch of what I call bad American habits, and I am sure I haven't even identified many yet to come.

I am incredibly lacking in this area, as I did not grow up anywhere else, obviously. I did not travel the world. I have not spent free time, created by wealth, becoming "cultured." I have read a few books and heard a few things though. There is an obvious different perspective in other countries compared to our American perspective. There are very clear patterns, usually joked about on social media. When seemingly every other country does something another way, in America we choose to do things that are obviously much more complicated, evidently hurt people, create problems, etc. Some obvious examples include pharmaceutical, medical, social, dietary, and political differences.

I do not have an answer. Let me tell you that too! The answer, or a quest to find the answer, is well beyond my reach. Mostly by choice... I choose not to be a part of that whole mess, as much as I can possibly avoid it. I choose to fight off the trickle-down effects that so many get stuck in. I have decided that I can change my American perspective of life, along with the roll over affects it has on my teaching career.

Within our shared and skewed American perspective, we still see things a bit differently. Every different position in a school has its own perspective. Each school climate creates a lens to look through to develop those perspectives. And each eyeball, looking through those lenses, has a unique background that makes them see it all in a different array of colors.

In other words, my perspective is no better or worse than anyone else's, but I do believe it to be unique. I do think my perspective matters and mostly because of things outside of teaching. I think my life experiences have put me in a position to see what others do not. I have also intentionally put an incredible amount of time into seeing what I had not before. This 'both sides' approach has vastly broadened my perspective. *Many have told me over the years that I am not a regular teacher. Deep down, this is the biggest compliment I have received as a teacher.*

Before we speak about my perspective, let's look at some others' perspectives and how much they have had an influence on my own. Each grade level in teaching requires the right attitude from the teacher. As the ages increase a certain type of attitude, behavioral approach, classroom management, and more must change along with it. In essence, good teachers must kind of change for their audience. They must change their perspective lens to relate, build rapport, and see how to connect with their students. Let's start where the students start, in kindergarten.

Let me tell you something. Kindergarten teachers are the craziest, most daring, decorative, brightly colored, motley crew among us teachers. These people are supposed to teach these pant wetting, snot slobbering, crayon eating students the most fundamental important parts of learning. This fairy tale group of teachers even sing sweet little melodies throughout the day, to brainwash these young pupils into learning. I believe this group of teachers have a little grandmother in them, running the show. With so many other grade levels out there, I just don't understand why some pick this age group. I am grateful they do! This is the one grade I have never worked with, and I intend to leave it to those who have that skill.

I think grade school teachers are somewhere between the sweetest people on earth to the most forgetful, angry creatures still roaming. This teaching niche, grades 1 through 6, is wild. They literally see hundreds of students a day, often up to 30+ at a time. Talk about self-inflicted ADHD. I know I have a touch. Grade school teachers create, manage, and shut down chaos every single class period of the day. This group of teachers still must line up the kids and march them from one place to the next to avoid utter chaos. You can really tell a lot about a teacher on how they manage those lines. Grade school teachers seem to actually care about the bulletin boards in the hallway too. Weirdos!

As a special education resource teacher, I have a different perspective while teaching in the grade school years. I get to hear all the stories, from the students, about those teachers. I get to look through the students' eyes. I get to know the teachers' personalities, from inside their classroom and out, in a unique and sometimes rehabilitating way. I then get to walk in the halls and do my thing, my magic to help those students and teachers.

Some grade school teachers have made me feel so special each time I walk into the room. I like to imagine they do this for all their students too. Others have made it hard for me to come to work; some teachers just look mean. I can only imagine how the students feel. It also seems these grades are filled with the most power tripping teachers. Seems these grade level teachers still use height and weight, along with the curriculum, as a grade of superiority. Watching teachers at this grade level get mad at kids for being kids has been incredibly hard for me to deal with over the years. It really feels like they have forgotten their own behavior at that age. Or unknowingly they have lost their willpower, leading to emotionally driven punishments rather than natural consequences.

I loved teaching these grades. A huge part of my perspective comes from working with these ages. I could act like the inner child I am and blame it on trying to make connections with my students. I could go play basketball or soccer at recess and break a kid's ankles. Or more likely, get stuffed by a tall 6th grader and hear about it in the halls for a few weeks. Teaching at this grade allowed me to do the same thing I did as a kid to get through the day, play. If teachers at this level can start to approach teaching a bit more from the kids' perspective, rather than the school boards, everyone would have fuller cups. Teachers and students alike will enjoy the experience, and the effects will continue through the educational experience.

Middle school teachers, how I spent much of my time teaching, are of course adults who have forgotten to grow up. They are kind of a perfect mix of grade school combined with high school, that uncomfortable transition. Good middle school teachers are weird! These teachers are filled with the stupidest of dad jokes. They are more excited for Halloween and other holidays than the students most times. Middle school teachers dye their hair after losing a bet to their homeroom class.

These teachers still have the hope that they can save a kid. Sometimes this age feels like the last chance to make a difference before they turn into full-grown terror teenagers in high school.

The only hard part about teaching middle school, for me, was that the students usually passed me in height. Right around 8th grade is where this 42-year-old man will admit, I can't keep up with them any longer. Parts of my body just don't move that fast anymore. As silly as it sounds, my 5'6" height has always been advantageous for me. I have watched teachers try to use their adulthood, height, stature to intimidate kids into learning. I am not into that at all.

I am a big advocate for teachers to learn that you cannot make anyone do anything. Some teachers think they can and practice it often. Slow down, take a deep breath. Kneel to a student's level, speak to them softly, show them the respect that you want, so they can learn it. Oh, how often do I watch the teachers break the exact rules that they yell at their students about. Always!

So many teachers either talk to peers, don't pay attention, or are on their phones during every staff meeting. It is quite comical, until you point it out to a middle school teacher. It is this group of teachers that argue the most too; they argue with students, with peers, with superiors, and with themselves. Such a huge waste of energy. What a terrible way to empty your cup. If you find that you don't have enough patience left for your students acting like kids, you are wasting your willpower on something else. If you find yourself frustrated about reexplaining a silly concept from your curriculum, you are losing willpower somewhere that you shouldn't be. Slow down, relax. Save some of that willpower for anything else.

Then there is High school; these teachers, so specific in their area of instruction, most times really are the most professional of teachers. I know a few who are kind of professional. Professionals by day and partiers by night, more like it. High school teachers must deal with little adult wannabes, all hyped up on hormones. Adrenal stress hormones, growth hormones, sex hormones, and so much more influences the daily decisions of these students. It takes a certain kind of patience, unlimited understanding, and strong flexible leadership to be a high school teacher. A good high school teacher, that is.

Oh yes, don't forget the rest of the high school teachers. These teachers are simply reliving their own high school lives, because they were so disappointed the first time or didn't know how to move into a career. Highschool teachers are sometimes the most invested and mascot like for their schools. These types of teachers are die hard and so confident in something they really cannot explain and then complain about almost always. Sorry, but another evidently true pattern.

Personally, I struggled at all big public high schools as a teacher, because I struggled when I was in these types of schools as a student. I don't like the feeling of high school people trying to be like the high school actors they have seen on television. Highschool just feels so fake to me. The bigger the school, the more fake it feels. It is where the rat race begins, and the many ladders are presented for those to climb. I have learned there is no way for me to change it, so I avoid it. This simply is not my niche in teaching. I belong to a different, smaller crowd.

If you haven't burned the book yet, settle down. I have lived the life of every one of these perspectives. Well, as mentioned, not kindergarten; that's crazy. I am so definitely scared of kindergarteners and put high praise on those teachers who have turned a kindergarten classroom from herding rabbits into a learning environment. All the different teaching perspectives are so important. They add up to the feelings, the actions/motives, and the culture of our schools.

Chapter 6 - Why My Perspective Matters

I almost didn't write this chapter because it felt kind of conceited. It felt like writing about my journey was selfish and a waste of time to other hard-working teachers. I decided to go ahead with it because the reason my perspective might matter is not because of something great I did. It is quite the opposite. My perspective is maybe worth hearing because of a whole lot of nots. What I was not, what I am not, and what I will not become.

First, my perspective is mentionable, because I was not an outstanding student. Anyone I went to school with that finds out about my career is incredibly surprised; it just doesn't make sense to them that I am now teaching. I was kicked out of one school and dodged the second consequence because of some great teachers and forgiveness. I was a little bit of a troublemaker, some may say. Others, like understanding, loving, good teachers, might just say I was a kid.

Also, I was not raised by teachers. I do not have teaching genetics passed down on either side of the family. It seems there is one of these teachers at every school I have ever worked at. The "my mom was a teacher, my grandmother was a teacher, my aunt is a teacher, my brother's sisters' father's best friend was a teacher." That kind of thing. I was not inspired to become one, by one amazing life changing adult in my student experience either, though I did have some great teachers along the way. Me becoming a teacher happened completely by accident. A beautiful little masterpiece of an accident.

After high school I went to community college, just because I wanted to further my soccer career and my girlfriend at the time was attending the same college. Love takes us in many different directions. My love of soccer and my girlfriend had me staying in school for no real reason. I had absolutely no direction and was super uncomfortable trying to further my education. Soccer kept me going, just as it did in high school. I still disliked learning at this point; and now looking back, I know why. I was made to learn so much that didn't relate to my life, it really didn't interest me. It was the random circumstances of following my girlfriend into college and not failing classes to play soccer that truly kept me going. Eventually it was my girlfriend's mother that tricked me into the unknown. She was a teacher and as we neared the end of coasting through community college, with no direction, she suggested it to both of us. She suggested we follow her down the path of teachership. I listened. Who knows why?

I later graduated from ASU. I was never anything special of a student here either, though I did start to enjoy learning at this point. They gave me some kind of yellow rope to hang over my shoulder, but truly, I never really tried to be a great student. I didn't really understand the joy of learning at the time, I just had nothing else to do. The only 2 reasons I was in college in the first place had dwindled away. I had torn both my ACL's and therefore my dream of becoming a soccer player was basically crushed. And my dang girlfriend dumped me. It was time to move forward into this world of adulthood, get a degree, have student debt, and then work the rest of my life to pay it off. It was time for me to move into what this degree said I was, A TEACHER.

Back then it wasn't like now; there was actual competition in the teaching market. I couldn't find a job after graduation. No one really needed a history teacher at the time, and I thought that was what I was. That is what my degree told me I was. I had been trained to do what a history teacher must do. (Weird side note looking back - I had avoided special education while in college, though it was suggested several times)

As I searched and waited for a teaching gig, the only job that hired me was home care for adults with disabilities. This was not only incredibly ironic but drove me even further from my comfort zone. This temporary get me through job was opening my eyes to a whole new perspective. Life's undesigned path showed me some strengths I never knew I had. I was finding a niche from just teaching in life, well after the degree that I paid so much money for. The schools may not have wanted me, but there were many people willing to be taught; a group of people I had neglected. Though college may have sparked some synapsis for me, I learned more about teaching well after going to school for it.

I intentionally did not do special education in my first years of college because I feared it. I feared the disabilities. I was afraid of everything I didn't know. I just didn't know any better. My mind knew nothing of the magic, the miracles, and growth that occurs outside the comfort zone. It was my simple ignorance that made me afraid of special education teaching. But at the time I had this "non-education" job that pointed in that very direction.

On top of the new job, I also started a whole new sport. In the most random of circumstances, I found myself riding bulls. I had no idea how much bull riding was going to teach me about persistence, teaching, life, comfort zones, effort, etc. All these things happened at the same time for me, which was huge to further open my perspective. Then it all made sense one afternoon, as if it was planned out.

Out of the blue, a friend from college called me up and asked if I had found a job yet. I told her no and she hooked me up with what she called, "kind of weird, but I think you would be great at it." I finally had landed my first teaching job which would last for the next decade and beyond my perspective, totally change my life. I was finally living the good life, with a salary of 37k. I had made it as a teacher!

This first teaching job of mine combined with my non-typical life experiences is the next reason I mention my lens. I spent the first 9 years of teaching, working for a service level D private placement school for students with behavioral needs. I was working in special education! I even went back to school. I was back in graduate school, getting my special education cross-categorical degree.

That first teaching gig had me working with students who were transported from multiple districts across the metropolitan of Phoenix. We had such a different array of students from so many different backgrounds. Every single day provided a new fire to put out, with very little water and an empty fire extinguisher. Day after day seemed impossible, but day after day we persevered through it. As mentioned earlier, this created a bit of a super-man complex in me. Working in this one school, with one population of students, felt more like working with the entire world. This is where I started to experience every grade level and every walk of life as a teacher, janitor, social worker, administrator, coach, and more. Everything except that daunting kindergarten classroom down the hall. The screams, the smells, the humanity. So many reasons to walk the other way. It seemed our "hats" pointed in every direction those days, which quickly taught me what college did not.

The non-educational, nontypical reason I want to share my story, and maybe my last chance to impress me another buckle bunny, is now that I was riding bulls, I believed in the impossible. For those of you who do not know this term "buckle bunny". It is those beautiful country ladies with the shiny assed jeans who are attracted to the latest winner of the buckle. Or in some cases those ladies attracted to whatever is attached to the buckle; no matter how fake a cowboy is who wears it. I am no cowboy either; I just spent almost a decade trying to ride bulls. There is a difference. To get us back on point, bull riding made me believe in the impossible. Truly, it was the most miraculously filled time of my life.

Twice a week I rode bulls, practiced and competition; riding with and against some people that had done this since they were children. I started riding at age 26, after tearing ACL's in both my knees along with some of those other supportive ligaments in there. Stupid soccer and all that damn running, cutting back and forth, and such. I thought my athletic career was over after my soccer injuries. It was those injuries that made me realize I wasn't going pro; I had to make money with some other job. I really had to be a teacher at that point. However, the injuries didn't stop me in this new sport the way they hindered me in soccer. There was still hope for my athletic career, along with a million new ways to hurt myself.

I had never really thought my brother and I's childhood dream of riding bulls would happen. We had the greatest of times, at first pretending, and eventually becoming bull riders. We made some life-long friends and earned some really great stories to tell. We were never the best, but that chapter was most certainly one of the best times of my life.

I was living the impossible in my personal/athletic life and that had a strong influence on my teaching style. We watched videos of me riding on the smart board in class; it was one of the few reasons I learned how to use that damn thing. I had a poster of me riding on the wall and students often had to hear about my latest success or mostly failures each week.

The truth was most of them loved the stories. It helped me and them distract ourselves from the daily rigor of school life. Bringing bull riding, my personal passion, into the classroom allowed me to make it longer than most starting teachers. It also had another amazing effect. *I believed in the impossible for me and my students. I still do.* I preached it to them every day from behind my pulpit, limping from the night of riding before. Some of the other staff and students started to believe it too. It felt like I found charisma by combining my love of sport with my job. I was so consistent and so passionate, so believable. I almost never missed work and quickly gained a reputation as a workaholic, anal retentive, perfectionist type among the staff. To some of the students, I was a hero. Sometimes, I even felt like one.

It felt good! This approach of mine worked and it didn't. My classroom management was and still is to this day amazing. Dealing with kids that don't want to be there is just where I come from. I was becoming an entertainer in front of the students, loaded with a tool belt of "off the wall" teaching strategies that could reach almost every student that entered my room. However, the same consistency, hard work, etc. that I used for my classroom had a different influence in other places.

Some of my peers despised me, though they came to me for help all the time. Usually behind my back, they complained or gossiped as so many teachers do. Work friends would try to help me get through as they told me what the "others" thought. (The clicks that exist in schools are just as strong amongst teachers as they are with the students) It was so hard to work next to people, help and lead people who did not have as much work effort as me. Sometimes I just didn't have enough patience for the adults I was surrounded with. We only have so much willpower...

I wasted so much willpower focusing on bad teachers. At certain points, I wasn't even able to hide it. I would lose it with what I deemed incompetent staff. It was a weird thing to be so effective and patient with the students yet often encouraged by my bosses to be more flexible with the staff. I am talking about staff who came to work only 60% of the time and lost their cool with kids in physical managements. I was asked to be more flexible with staff who talked shit to kids, acted as terrible role models, and just were not good people in my eyes. It was very hard for me to work so diligently in my bull riding career, my daily life, and my career as a teacher, while surrounded by some people who didn't work hard at anything. I still struggle to this day, but I am certainly working on it by trying to turn a blind eye.

I only mention this struggle because it is a critical part of my lens. I think learning to give less attention to these types of coworkers is an important piece to how to become a recovering teacher. *I am learning that may just be the way it is, AND I will not waste my willpower on it. The critical addition of not caring about what we cannot control is an important part of the equation.* Good teachers, especially, think they control too much. I did. My super-hero complex from all my past accomplishments told me so. Turns out, I was wrong, wrong, wrong.

These "wonder years" of my teaching career led to me being on so many different campuses across Arizona, I don't have a count. Just like them buckle bunnies for a couple years there. LOL Eventually, I helped open and run our satellite campuses within a few different districts. This time as a teacher was the most rewarding and so unlike what most teachers get caught up with. I was gaining a critical, experienced, confident lens to make decisions for my future career. It prepared me for all that happened next.

A lot of different circumstances, irrelevant to the point, led to me leaving the private realm of teaching. Mostly, my company sold out and was led by some corporate fellas I could not stand. I could not stand them so much that I jumped ship, another critical step to the equation. My perspective was about to become even clearer, as I moved into what so many told me was the teacher's dream and it even came with benefits and a state retirement plan.

I decided to move into the public realm, where promises were made by a principal who was fired for having the guts to speak up that very next year. She had a heart to follow her own trail, rather than the school board's treasure map. She was one that did not accept that is just the way it is. I have not met many principals who still have their guts and heart, especially in the public realm of education. Most public-school administrators and principals are just a bunch of puppets on a string, winners of a popularity contest. Thank you for cutting those strings, to all the principals who stay true to themselves! To the rest of you leaders who are terribly offended right now, I really do not mean to do so. There are patterns among you leaders too, which a recovering teacher needs to learn to avoid.

Basically, we have three types of principals in school districts. First, there are the power tripping, I climbed the ladder type. The kind that loves to tell about their own miraculous stories of the past, rather than listen. These principals are great at holding teachers responsible for things out of their control and making them feel bad about it. Too many teachers have come to me crying, complaining, or mostly cursing about these kinds of principals. This group of leaders are so politically driven by the school board and have more interest in the business side of teaching to think for others or themselves. They are puppets, trying to puppeteer anyone else who will listen.

Next, we have the I am going to change the world type of administrators. This second type of administration style is outright draining to watch. Usually, this person is newer to the position still filled with young blood and ignorance. They are put into the worst of schools, encouraged with bonuses, promises, and future retirement bumps. These leaders are climbing the ladder for sure, but still have a true bleeding heart. A dangerous combination. This second type will listen, will relate with you, will even care. However, this type of leader is still too scared to make a difference. Too scared to shake the ladder and fall off. On top of that, these leaders are so drained, with their hands tied behind their backs, they do not have the energy to truly help staff fill their cups. These types of principals come off too fake to me. I also seem to get a contact high from the coffee or energy drinks they are usually hyped up on. Personally, these types of leaders make me feel anxious. This group of leaders mean well, but usually leave their staff wanting and needing more.

Last, there are the leaders that make a difference. There are those principals that swing by your room to tell you jokes, rather than check in. They pay so much attention to their staff; they know when to help and when to leave things alone. When butting heads with these types of leaders, both people come out stronger. My principal took me to lunch in the middle of the day to try to help me realize I was not that important. *He really tried to teach me to be a better person, not a better teacher. Good leaders are hard to find because they are hard to become, especially in the revolving door of education.* I have had a few true mentors over the years, that really made a difference in my life, rather than my career. Most of them were not in leadership positions. Hats off to the administrators who wore their many hats well!

Again, I do not mean to offend administrators. I am just pointing out the patterns that have been shared from your teachers' mouths. I am speaking super directly from my own opinion too, of course, but to offer you another choice. If any one position could make a difference by *not* accepting that is just the way it is mentality, it could be the principal position. Good principals influence in all directions, with students, with teachers, parents, board members, and much more. A huge thank you to those leaders, along the way, that proved to me it is possible!

In accordance, I hope many of you get to see this book and know how much you are appreciated and remembered by not only this fella, but all those students. I have worked with some of the greatest human beings, as a teacher. I have also worked with some of the biggest-hearted people in this world; the kind that get you through those real crappy days. Artists, musicians, professional athletes, and more have luckily crossed my educational path. I have seen the most "non-typical" teachers over the years. It has been such a pleasure to work with non-programmed, no degree, undereducated teachers being good teachers just the same.

I struggled with this at one point, thinking why the hell did I pay for college? I looked down on some of the best teachers in the world for some very wrong reasons. I now realize, it is the actions over the degree that really makes a teacher. I'm still pissed about my student loans... LOL

Watching other teachers show students love, patience, and empathy made me realize where I wanted to use my willpower at work. Without the incredible experiences shared with these colleagues over 15 years, my perspective would be so boring. Again, I consider it the biggest compliment when students say I am not a regular teacher. I never wanted to be regular at anything.

Public school's path led me astray for 3 years, until I finally could not stand following bad leadership and my own silly patterns. I was literally going crazy at the time, thinking that the rest of my career was going to continue the same way. Without paying attention to my own crazy, I may never have left. This may be another reason I think my perspective is important; I will happily get fired, more readily quit if my values begin to be compromised. By the way, I have never been fired. I am too good of a teacher... LOL I am also happy to move on from places that I do not belong, no matter how much money and "comfortable" retirement is promised.

On top of escaping the public realm, I am learning not to waste my time at work with the rat race, popularity contest, people pleasing type stuff that happens amongst adults. I am learning to use my willpower in the right direction and not waste as much as possible, in my own unique way. I used to, but I no longer need to impress others. I will still kick your butt on the pool table when challenged. I will defend my position with some expressive rhetoric when debated. I will show you test scores, progress reports, student growth, etc. if you make me. I still can impress when I need to. I am just not going to do it at work, unless it's for the students and families. I am learning to be less of a people pleaser to save my will power for the whole reason I am a teacher. To help the kids grow up...

I seemingly ran the whole teaching gauntlet, tried to quit and now landed a job, through a contract company. Oh wait... LOL before that, the only reason I made it into contract teaching was because my attempt to quit teaching, all together, didn't stick...

After I walked away from the district gig, I stayed in Minnesota with my dad for one summer just to see what would happen. Without effort, in an accident, almost miraculously, I got a construction job with a friend and absolutely loved it. There was a type of freedom I had not felt in all my years of teaching. There was something great about working with my hands too. I was sore in my body, rather than my mind. I could see the positive results right in front of me day to day, where sometimes you just don't get that in special education teaching.

"Holy Shit", I said to myself one day. "I have recovered." At the time, I was throwing some mud on the wall trying to fix my wide cracks in the sheet rock, while singing along with some country music on the radio. I have followed the Applebee's man path right out of education into a brand-new career, I thought to myself. I was about 5 months in and kind of getting the hang of things. As much as I thought this new job was my path to recovering teacher, it was not. It wasn't the sore back. It wasn't the uncomfortably feeling of a new job. I really don't know what it was. It just happened. My perspective still had room to grow.

Eventually, I saw the geese head south in that most beautiful formation. I saw it so many times, over and over, on my wintry hikes; it seemed symbolic each time. The geese told me it was time to go home. And then the cold of Minnesota in December. The cold might be what really sent me back south. Those folks living up in that weather are as crazy as kindergarten teachers! Something called from back home in the southwest, though I couldn't clearly hear what it was. So, I shed the layers of warm clothes as I drove back south.

When I made it back to Arizona, I did not plan on returning to teaching. I looked for another job that would provide the same freedom I had found in Minnesota. Part of the American dream that I am aware of and incredibly grateful for. It just didn't work out. Surprisingly, maybe not, teaching was going to be the best paying job for me at the time. With my little experience in construction the pay was low, the companies were slow to hire, and full of a bunch of meatheads that I had no desire to be around. I investigated a lot of jobs that would keep me recovering. I even applied and then chickened out from the offer of being a waste management technician. Looking back, I was obviously going through a midlife crisis in my educational career.

It was mid-January then; many schools needed teachers, and my new contract company got me some good money per hour. This was my first experience with contract teaching. I had seen these creatures walking through the halls of our schools in past years, but I knew nothing about contract teaching. Looking back, I should have held out for more money. Schools were, and are still, in desperate need of good teachers. It turns out that's what I am. No matter how I tried to run from it, I was meant to be a teacher, and I am damn good at it. I am a hard worker out of habit, just like my mother and so many others that taught me to be the way I am. So much of my early life, my American dream, simply led in the direction of teaching. A programming I could not undo, or at least that's what I told myself while I walked back into that school feeling like a million bucks.

The return to teaching was triumphant as I quickly became one of the "favorite" teachers on campus again. It was different in one outstanding way. Now it felt like I was the favorite of both students and staff. Not because I was special or anything. I was surrounded by overworked, brainwashed, burnt out teachers that needed help. They needed my help. I was fresh and ready from my time away and filled with something new. They were all about to jump ship it seemed, barely holding on, but not me. This return to the teaching world brought me closer every day to becoming a recovering teacher. I didn't know it, but I now had a new superpower growing inside me.

I found myself back in the classroom, now as a resource teacher with 3rd and 4th graders. Maybe one of my favorite jobs as a teacher, even though we were understaffed, and it was well outside my regular niche. It was here that I started to practice *my* version of recovery. It was this experience with my first contract position that the light bulb went off just a little brighter. I was told not to go to after-school meetings. I was offered overtime pay for anything done before or after school hours. My company often fought for me. They fought for me not to do things I used to think were a necessary part of my job. It created some very direct rays of light in the dark areas of my teaching past. It showed me a different path that eventually I learned to make my own.

During my teaching resurrection, I continued to talk to people about my book, this idea of recovery. Each person I spoke with at work, and at the bar, was incredibly supportive and interested. One of the main reasons this book is finished is the support received from colleagues, friends, and strangers along the way. The patterns that I had realized so many years ago were still there, but I wasn't a part of them. At that point, I really felt the need to finish this book. Working as a contract worker allowed me the extra time to do just that, as it also broadened my perspective.

The last reason I think my perspective is important is that I am 15 years into the profession as a special educator. I worked 11 years in a self-contained classroom setting and 4 years as a resource teacher. I have worked with almost every grade level at more schools than I can remember the count. I have traveled to an array of different schools and experienced more than any teacher should in my short career. Oh yeah, I worked at a night school for a couple years too. I have spent 15 diverse years in the teaching business, all the time learning to change. This is the perfect amount of time to balance certain feelings that may arise in any career. More importantly, this is the perfect amount of time to realize what patterns help you as a teacher and which patterns you can break free from.

I am not so deep into teaching that I have given up swimming, though I did try. I am not so deep as to believe that this is just the way it is, to drown with everyone else. *No one person or group of people has guilted me into feeling I need to stay anywhere either.* I am also not so green as to have an outspoken dream, filled with ignorance. I am not just holding on at my first rodeo, hoping the bull comes out weak that night. I am at this comfortable middle point in my teaching timeline. I can look forward and backward at the same time, without crashing. My teaching lens is unique, as I walk through schools as a contracted resource teacher. It is sometimes almost as peaceful as the woods.

Chapter 7 — Well Beyond My Perspective

Why would anyone work a job that requires them to go in early and stay late that never pays overtime? Why develop carpel tunnel with all those papers to staple and emails to send? Who in their right mind would work a job where many of those you serve are ungrateful? Who in the world would choose to go back year after year to have everything changed from the year before? Then expected to do it all over again, but even better. I say year, but these changes are weekly in special education - with schedules, new students, meetings with all kinds of acronyms. Hell, we even had meetings about meetings. Why would anyone choose to be a teacher with so many other higher paying careers and jobs out there?

One of these silly folks just happens to be my best friend. This teacher, who turned principal, has the most bleeding heart I have ever seen amongst us teachers. He provided snacks, prize incentives, gift cards, and BBQ's all out of his own pocket for the small charter school he led as principal. Spending money doesn't make you a good teacher, but it seems to be a popular thing in the profession. When the school won't do it, someone does, teachers like this guy and I am sure a bunch of you. Well beyond the money, this incredibly hard-working man works way over the 40 hours a week, like most teachers. Before he was principal, he went in on the weekends to make sure his lesson plans were done. LOL Lesson Plans. Don't get me started. After becoming principal, he still went in on the weekends to do whatever those people do at schools "to teach kids" on the weekend. LOL This idiot friend of mine has declined camping trips over and over, because he must catch up on work.

My best friend has gone well beyond working hard, for school. He has allowed two graduated, struggling, ex-students to live with him and get them both jobs to help after graduation. This man gave everything to his students and his school, until the school pushed too far. After being asked to fudge numbers in a ridiculous fashion, my best friend quit teaching after 15 years. He was so hurt by the institution that this most loving, big hearted person quit teaching all together. Well, just like me... he tried. He lasted only about a year, working side jobs and bartending, until he was sucked back into the education world. This is the kind of person who teaches. This is the kind of person who is back to working so damn hard, I can barely get one camping trip a year from him. I preferred his other schedule. LOL That is the perspective that exists in good teachers, that is my best friend!

Here's another perspective. Let's talk about my sister, who worked as a paraprofessional for many years in the special education realm. She was the webster dictionary definition of a good teacher. She worked harder than her lead teacher every single day. Like many paraprofessionals, my sister made up for what this teacher did not do. And when that teacher quit, the school used my sister as the lead teacher to finish out the year. My sister was not monetarily compensated for everything she did extra, but her heart told her to keep giving. She had many real complaints and crazy stories to share, but she never even thought of quitting. When I told her to speak up for herself, she said she was doing it for the kids. If my sister did as much for herself as she does for others, she would rule the world. She just isn't that type. Don't worry though, she did get out of teaching to become a nurse. LOL This is the kind of person who gets into teaching, people with too big of hearts. That's the perspective that so many teachers have, that's my sister!

I have heard a few teachers over the years mention adoption. Some of the greatest kids out there don't have any parents. When these kids find their way into your classroom it's kind of like being covered in fairy dust, by Tinkerbell. I don't know. It makes some emotions come alive that make a person want to save the world; makes you feel like you could fly. I even thought about adopting a student once myself. I quickly snapped back to reality after sobering up the next day. Year after year I heard this pattern from school to school. One year, a teacher walked into my room and said she was doing it. About 2 months later, she actually did it! She was already a parent of 3, with so many things going on. And if I do dare say it, she had enough going on to where she could probably spend more time figuring that out. Instead, she adopted this most needing kid. She did it! I assume she couldn't stop herself. This is the kind of person who becomes a teacher!

I have asked at least 100 teachers over the years, "What makes you keep teaching? You cannot say the students." The poetic answers that rang back, which only could be sprung from the mouth of a teacher, were beautiful... and strung out. I became so sick of the repeated rhetoric after just a dozen or so interviews that I had to change my question. I changed the question to better fit my grading rubric, as only a veteran teacher knows how to do. "The answer can only have one word", I told them. This saved me from some of the never-ending conversations, but the answers still had repeated patterns. Hope, faith, love, summer were a few answers that stuck out. However, the answer that most frequently popped up was passion.

Now I don't want to poke fun at these folks, many of them friends and colleagues of mine, but I must point out some realities. I need to show what loving eyes too often overlook. These teachers that answered my question with the tongues of an angel are the same teachers that do the following.

These articulate boasters of passion are the same teachers that post on social media about how well-deserved their vacation time is just a few weeks back from the last break. These same apparently self-deprived workers post how long it has been since they treated themselves. These educational martyrs are the same that complain at happy hour, way too many times a week, about this student and that student. Using code names to follow FERPA, of course.

These passion filled workers have so little passion left, they spend the after-work hours super binging on the most popular Netflix shows. It comes up about a dozen times a day, mostly with teachers who have run out of things to complain about. "Have you seen this show, that show, you need to watch this, etc." Too many teachers live the life of that's just the way it is every day, so caught up in the patterns they never see the effects at work or at home. These are the real patterns and feelings of teachers shared outside their fantasy.

These most loving people are the same teachers who refuse to have children! I have heard the words, "I don't want kids.", "I hate kids", or something similar way too many times from teachers. The same overworked folks who cannot work out because they're exhausted at the end of the day say that passion keeps them doing the job of teaching. The list goes on and on. *These supposedly passion filled folks seem to only use their passion to deal with work.* They overuse their passion just because that is the way it is at work. Or maybe, our passion is misguided and abused by an unstoppable system.

All these teachers had such great things to say about why they teach when asked with the right lighting, but the reality at the job place and the aftereffects of the job were and are much the opposite. If you asked them a little differently and at a different time, there may be a little more realistic truth into their statements. They would mention how bad the new teaching curriculum is or how underfunded the schools are. They would certainly point out the overcrowded classroom. Some would complain about their incompetent coworkers or ignorant leaders. If prompted with the right questioning, most teachers would point out the impossibilities that they are put through much too often. Many would say they are currently looking for another job. New teachers would lie to themselves and say it's just a temporary hardship of the learning curve. Older, "more experienced" teachers would say that's just the way it is. When responding honestly in the day to day, most teachers complain about the job way before they express that passion.

I will point out that I am on some of these lists, of course. As a recovering teacher, I am on less of these lists. I am working on breaking many of these same old habits. There is no judgement at all...

Okay, there is a little judgment, but with a finger pointed both at you and me. I often love to tell non-teachers about the great things I have accomplished as a teacher. I happily entail the one-of-a-kind stories that only a teacher could experience in many conversations. There is something fantastic about the responses from others about how great you are at dealing with and helping all those kids. I am for sure guilty of this self-martyrdom. It was this very perspective that I needed to find in myself to work on it. This leads us to our next chapter.

Chapter 8 - The Social Emotional Benefits Catch

I believe in social emotional benefits in the workplace. I believe that teachers get some of the greatest and most frequent social emotional benefits compared to many of the jobs out there. Of course, nurses, maybe some doctors, paramedics, and missionaries may experience some of these same types of benefits... But no other job truly finds minute-to-minute social interactions, like teaching. In no other career do you experience so many emotions attached to so many relationships as in the education career.

For a good teacher who is aware, there are an abundant number of benefits well beyond state retirement money, health, dental, 401K and all that jazz. I don't believe there is another job out there that can compare. Truly, I don't know if there is a comparison job out there, because I have not worked in another career. Nevertheless, I would happily compare and debate with any other job that the social emotional benefits in teaching are more.

Some of you may not even be aware of the social emotional benefits that you are experiencing day to day. Too caught up in work responsibilities first, then the phone, and then life... to feel those most important feelings. There is a chance that I am making it up too, but I am pretty sure I heard of social emotional benefits somewhere.

In this author's perspective, a social emotional benefit is the non-monetary, non-physical value that one gains by working one's job. Just like it sounds, it is the social and emotional growth that one can gain from their daily life on the job.

For instance, a bartender gets to hear some of the best/worst stories and jokes while on the job. A bartender learns to talk, listen, and act as a therapist, sometimes willingly behind the bar. A good bartender becomes better at these things over the years because of these experiences; both at their workplace and in life. These skills from the "nine to five" hours can carry over into our everyday actions. Bartenders become different people because of these social emotional benefits at work. This is a social emotional benefit.

Similarly, a salesman gets to learn the art of talking, sometimes the art of listening. Long-time sales folks become completely caught up with making a sale that they try to sell their family members, friends, etc. well past the job. Salesmen could become great communicators because of their job requirements.

In some jobs, traveling becomes a social emotional benefit from the world experiences. All the experiences from the job add up to who that person becomes. The hardworking traveler may overlook how many architectural wonders, goofy accents, fantastic delicacies they get to enjoy that others do not, just because their job requires travel. The observant hard-working traveler soaks it all up and becomes "more cultured" as a benefit of working.

Construction workers or other labor type jobs can lead to a nice physique, strong body, great knowledge for owning a home, and terrible back pain when older. LOL Discount that last one. Construction workers on a roof leads to a nice tan. Hell, all the construction workers I know are the best shit talkers out there. Any job, of course, can teach so much more than just the obvious simple things that apply at work. But certain jobs simply stand out, actively teaching the employee additional values along the way. These are what this author calls social emotional benefits.

For a teacher, the social emotional benefits are incredibly diverse. From my point of view, teachers can gain presentation, speaking, and listening skills among a few. Furthermore, a good teacher learns feelings of sympathy/empathy, insight into poverty, and insight into so many lives never lived. Teachers learn how to lead and parent, whether they are good at it or not.... I personally learned honesty, humility, forgiveness, the computer skills I should have learned long ago, patience, and so much more. A teacher gets the same salesmanship benefits trying to sell their lesson every day. They also get some of the bartender benefits as they find themselves at the bar every night; joking of course. Kind of.... Just like bartenders, teachers are telling jokes, acting as therapists, hearing some of the best and worst stories on a day-to-day basis. We pretend to listen to some super boring stuff, some really listen... and don't even get tips! Last, just like the traveling jobs benefits, the teacher gets the summers off to experience all those same exotic traveling experiences.

These social emotional benefits that come along with teaching are amazing. These benefits are comparable to a professional athlete taking home the championship title. There is an incredible feeling associated with working so hard for yourself and for others. Each graduation, promotion, grade advancement, etc. can feel like another lifetime achievement. These benefits can make a teacher feel like how the doctor must feel when they save someone's life. They have changed not only that one person's life but all of those who surround them. It feels dang good as a teacher to have people/strangers tell you time and again, "I could never do what you do." "You must be so patient." "God Bless you." This is the start of the social-emotional trap. For some people, most people in fact, it feels incredibly good to give. It makes a person want to just keep giving.

But let us take a broader view rarely ever seen by giving people. Let's look at the other side of this giving. Like anything, all the examples above also have some negative side effects. No matter how great winning the championship is, there are some lasting side effects that are irreversible. Professional sports can lead to some messed up joints down the road and some sacrifices made in their personal lives, with spouses, children, and more. Too much sacrifice can lead to much worse issues down the line, usually emotional.

Saving someone's life must almost make a doctor feel godlike. As a doctor it must feel incredible at the end of the day to know it started with you, except when it doesn't end with saving someone's life. I can only imagine the punishment good doctors put on themselves about things well out of their control.

Like a doctor, or an athlete, so many other jobs, and of course teaching, there is neglect in their personal life because of what they fail to neglect in their work life. Time is a hard thing to put value on if a person is not paying attention. Time is an impossible thing to get back.

The efforts that go toward our hardships, that add up to gaining social emotional benefits in our jobs, are outright draining. For me, looking back on the wasted time was something I recognized and didn't want to continue. As a teacher, I wanted to make sure I was investing and cashing in what so many were seemingly wasting.

Social emotional benefits are a huge part of anyone's job whether they know it or not; for teachers they can be life-changing or usually career-changing. These benefits also become part of what I call the social emotional catch. We get so caught up in the extra good feeling stuff we're doing, that other parts of our jobs or lives become more stressful. We voluntarily make our lives harder, some of us without any plan how to fix it. Many good teachers, unknowingly, make a habit of helping others so often, they completely empty their cups. They do it so habitually, they don't realize their help becomes less and less effective over time. We don't recognize when we need to take care of ourselves because the temporary satisfaction of helping others feels so good. We need it, like an unaware addict. The simple this for that exchange feels like it is filling our cup when it is really taking more and more.

Above the rest of these dangerous social emotional catches is the sympathy/empathy that teachers experience. Teachers, at least the ones who still care, can taste the hunger of their students. They can feel/hear the abuse from parents put down physically and emotionally to their children. I wonder if other teachers had a touch of some PTSD when trying to help students through their issues with a stepdad. I did...

Experienced teachers can see what lies down the road, good and bad, for so many of their students. Empathetic educators live the life of every one of their students while in the classroom and out. These social emotional catches can lead to a mind filled with much more than maybe the mind is capable. Crowded classrooms plus a caring teacher, combined with too many variables for this fellow, is a simple equation that equals a drained teacher.

Rather than thinking about our own family when we are at home, we are thinking about how to help our students. Instead of taking care of ourselves, we think about how much more we can do for a child that we will only know for one year, maybe a touch more. In place of everything teachers could do for themselves, family, friends, etc. the cup of willpower is spilled into circumstances that really, we cannot fix nearly as much as the things we can fix right at home. We really do waste so much willpower at work, no matter how good that temporary feeling.

As I started to balance those things at work, I tried to compensate for lost time with family and old friends. Of course, I had to share my ideas with them too. My best friend told me some of the ideas in my book were crazy and ignorant. As an ex-principal, current high school teacher returning from leaving the profession, he was telling me... lol. I just wanted to remind you of that. My best friend's perspective was that I was seeing from just my point of view and had neglected, "how much more rigor the general education realm required... how many more students general education teachers had...how much pressure principals were under." He was quick to try to point out my ignorance, but really, he was caught between the last chapter and this one. He was thinking this is just the way it is, and the social emotional catch was getting him through it, as do so many of us good teachers.

He said, like I heard so many others complain, that the school day didn't have enough hours to get work done, even with his "prep", going in early and staying late. He went on to say how important it was about being organized at work and how proud he was that he was the most organized he had been in years. He proved his point by saying he could only do all those things with the extra hours and effort he was putting in. He nailed it, "That's just the way it is." I felt bad when I bluntly asked him about his house project that was now taking years rather than months to complete. I felt even worse when I went deeper and pointed out some stuff in his love life he was going through at the time. Again, I felt even worse when he admitted he was compensating at work; he felt great at work, and he needed that at the time. He needed the social emotional trap to deal with the rest of life.

It reminded me of the many times that I needed that. I thought I needed that… Sometimes I still use those great work feelings to lift myself up at the end of a long week. It was at this point that I had to question my whole idea. I knew exactly what he was saying. Work makes me feel good sometimes too. Maybe we do need it? How can you even think that you should do less at work for all those students you love so much? It sounds insane.

As I drove home that night, it all made sense to me. I wasn't living up to my ideals to be there for my best friend when he needed me the most. I wasn't using my social emotional benefits outside of work like I could. I was no cashing in… I was still unbalanced, and I hadn't done for him what I was preaching about. How could he understand what I was still figuring out? We have barely dipped our toes into the water but let this be a little bit of a baptism for you.

As a practicing recovering teacher, I still cried with more students at school than with my own family and friends. There were some emotional students that year and sometimes I have reciprocating crying syndrome, RCS. I get it during some movies and really good commercials too. LOL

Even though I fought it, I still went way out of my way to help some of my colleagues almost every day. Even with the idea of recovering teacher in my head, I still did more than I should at work out of habit. And now I had started writing this book, spending even more time and effort in that direction.

No matter how busy I was, I saw my best friend here and there, of course. We talked, but not like I was talking with the students and parents about their futures. We both weren't talking about the most meaningful things in life, like we used to. My friend and I, unknowingly, neglected to talk about the things in life that bring about those tough emotions. We both did enough of that at work.

I couldn't tell him or show him what a recovering teacher was because I was still using so much willpower at work. I had just evolved my work away from school into the writing process and walking through the woods. I was still so deeply lost in some patterns that were holding back my own recovery.

My friend and I had found a distance between us that I didn't even realize was there. I knew more about what the students and coworkers of the time were going through, because that is where I still spent at least 8 hours a day. Even though I didn't bring that work home with me, *I wasn't making any time to work on some of my relationships.* It turned out I was still doing the same thing in my own new creative way. I was not using my social emotional investments wisely.

I was still caught up, so creative in making excuses to be busy all the time. *I was like a recovering addict who simply moved from one drug to another.* I was choosing to be so busy that I never had the time to hang out. I never made time for the good stuff. I didn't use my willpower enough for everything I was preaching about.

This was an enlightening moment right in the middle of writing this book. It showed me that I still had some room to recover myself, a lot of room. *It showed me that there is no such thing as recovered teacher, but always a recovering teacher.*

Looking back over the years, I can see this happened in multiple relationships of mine. This distance happened with my brothers, sister, mother, and father at different points too. I am certain I lost a girlfriend or two because I did not invest the same emotions with them that I did with students, day in and day out. No doubt there are many other factors that add up to healthy relationships. For me, using most of my time and efforts at work most certainly had an impact on the effort I was giving my family and friends.

It was another obvious pattern that I had found in myself and so many of my colleagues over the years. It was something I decided to stop making excuses about. We drain our cups of our social emotional powers and forget to use them on the most important people in our lives. It felt like I had wasted a whole lot of time, stuck in my own self-inflicted trap.

Chapter 9 - Finding a Balance

Teachers must learn to find a balance between work and life. No shit, Sherlock! You may be thinking this is the most obvious statement and it is. It is one of the most obvious things people continue to neglect day after day. We humans have so much trouble finding a balance between what we eat, when to go to sleep or wake up, what to say and not to say, and of course our phone use. Most folks have no time or energy to balance the rest of life or even recognize a need for it. The truth is, most rarely give themselves the time to figure any of this out. Others think they already have found balance, while they choose to walk a daily tightrope; often complaining about it. Because most create their own imbalance, it can be a hard thing for the person to admit and eventually see.

This balance will be different for everyone, of course, but it needs to be addressed, and it needs to be a daily practice for teachers. Without daily practices, there is a chance that recovery is not possible. Patterns are strong in schools and must be continuously broken to create new ones. I have fallen back into old teaching habits multiple times while writing this book. Each time I fought my way back out again, but only because I knew I could. I will mention again that these ideas could easily pertain to almost any job. Here, we address the desperate need for teachers to find their balance.

I know that there will be those teachers who read this, thinking about me as I thought about the Applebee's man. He can't hack it, he has no heart, etc. Some of you may say I am burnt out, just not dedicated, or as hard a worker as you. I will remind you, I am teaching today and doing it well. Walk into my classroom and watch the miracles that exist to this day. I have lost nothing and am nowhere close to being burnt out.

I just don't do it like so many of the rest of you; like I used to. I am figuring out my own balance, with work coming in second and sometimes third place after the rest of life. I am confident in recovering from a previous teaching style that was programmed into me as a good thing. I am a recovering teacher!

One general education teacher told me this idea of balance was just my ignorance as a special education teacher, like we have it easy. Again, this word ignorance was used to describe me; after 15 years of teaching... I swallowed my pride and listened to the reasons. I was told that as a special education teacher, I didn't understand the importance of grades and high standards for teaching... He thought just like my best friend. He said the exact same thing, as if it was programmed deep into him... I was told general education teachers had to do work at home to keep up with the rigorous demands of parents. This person believed that general education teachers had more grading and more students, etc. He continued that general education teachers had more pressure to keep their scores up from administration, well beyond the parents. He had a lot to say; nothing I had not heard before. His words were all echoes of a past pattern I was fighting off.

Part of what he and some others say is true for sure. *But that is a simple distraction, a sweet sleight of hand, from a much more profound point.* I like my niche in teaching; that is why I chose it. That is why I have fine-tuned it, to be where I belong... I don't want to work in general education for part of the reasons this pompous general education teacher was saying. This doesn't mean special education is easier. No matter what is involved with each position, they all have their own shit. *The shit is usually self-inflicted too.* I also do not want to be a teaching assistant, school secretary, or a principal. All these positions have their own related stress. These people do things I could never do... Much more accurately, they do the things I do not want to do.

For anyone still struggling with this idea, maybe thinking these ideas are crazy, consider these questions. Why would I ever choose a job that I am going to complain about? Why would I work somewhere that I do not like? Why do I have to do extra work at home? That is crazy, in my opinion.

I personally do not think any job is more difficult than another. We make daily choices that make our jobs easy or difficult for ourselves. We have control and make choices, even within all those terrible patterns that can exist in the workplace. The point is not comparing which job is more difficult. The point is how to deal with it and find your own balance in whichever position you have decided is yours.

Bus drivers, cafeteria staff, and office staff are all dealing with their own particular challenges. The bus driver has the lives of each child at stake, each morning and afternoon drive. That same driver needs to wake up from their nap for each afternoon route. LOL Cafeteria staff watch the kids make the same messes day in and day out. They then clean it up without so much of a thank you from most kids. I will admit that the cafeteria staff was one of my favorites to make quick friends with. Daily, they helped fill my cup... and my belly.

The school office is another great place to make friends. Office staff often wear so many hats, none of them ever fit right, but still they put them on. So many worn hats make for one hell of an interesting fashion show. Office staff are asked one day to fill in for the nurse and the next to talk down a distressed student. Office staff continue their daily odd tasks when they fill in for late staff and guide reckless parents through the pick-up line. They track every one of those little angels and report daily to the other side. Office staff connect the lives of so many unique, conflicting, weirdly separate worlds. I wouldn't trade.

Every position in school has too much to do. It is a part of the educational system; it is the business side of teaching. It is set up to get done with the least people possible, like any good business. In fact, it is a great business model making some folks rich... But let us not get into that whole mess.

For that specific argument coming from a general education teacher, special education does have a different set of demands, but they are just as challenging. *All teaching positions have their benefits and challenges in their own way, but most importantly, in their own equally treatable way.* All teaching positions are overloaded with too many responsibilities; do not convince yourself you are better than your peers because you try to get them all done. That is what I used to do, and it only leads to burning out. It is not the path for a recovering teacher.

This other teacher's perspective was so deep in, nothing I was saying could be heard. He continued to say I didn't understand the workload difference. I do understand the difference. There is none. I have made the decision to leave work at work, while others bring it home. I don't write IEP's while watching football on Sundays anymore. I don't lesson plan in the shower any longer, like a weirdo. On top of that, I am learning to not care about climbing the ladder, winning pieces of paper for whatever reward of the week/month, and any other silly shit. I am trying to make things better at work that I can, while letting go of the rest. There is so much more substance to life, and I am learning that I only have so much willpower to find it.

Nevertheless, I will try to answer his, and I am sure many others, debate. How can you just stop doing the work that is expected of you? How can you stop caring so much? You will get in trouble. You will get fired. LOL... That is true for you teachers who are still learning what work is. A portion of you need to be fired more readily, so you can learn a work ethic. Some of you should have been fired long ago...

Trouble and getting fired is so far from the truth for talented, caring, hard-working teachers. You are needed! You are recognized! You are also the most beautifully souled human being, working your ass off out of an unintended bad habit. You will not be fired for advocating for yourself. You will be freed from your own trap. You will not be let go or demoted for pointing out the systems' failures. You will more likely be thanked and promoted, tricked into the next level by a sly talking puppet.

More than likely, you will be forgiven or told to just keep doing your best. Good leadership will know that they shouldn't fire you. If they don't realize your worth, you shouldn't work there. Let them fire you, or walk away with some confidence, and move on to a new job that will appreciate you. It really can be that easy. Especially now, with such a heavy need in the career of teaching. There are so many ways to go about finding your balance.

Here is a very specific, and made to be, complicated example of finding balance in the teaching world. Let's take one of the most work loaded positions, the English teacher. English teachers could be considered the most actual over worked position due simply to the grading. In all other subjects, you can use straight forward methods to grade all the things you must. Multiple choice, fill in the blanks, poster projects, etc. Be honest folks. History, Math, Science, and electives are so much easier to grade than the huge number of full papers/essays that English teachers "read" and grade. And let's be honest English teachers; we know at a certain point your reading turns to skimming, then to a glance, often followed by sleeping. It is literally impossible for English teachers to do all their grading at school. So, some of you (most of you) may say they need to take that work home. Nope!

Recovering teacher says English teachers should get two preps. Give employees the time to do their job, while at work. If not, give them the teaching assistant to support this grading, or at least pay the teacher more money. If not that, hire more English teachers and give them less students each. Seems simple to me. There are many other solutions. As some of you are stuck in "that's just the way it is", I say no! Find another answer. Figure out another way. Avoid the sacrifice for the right reasons. Rather than reading papers at the dinner table, neglecting to talk with your own family, leave work in the school building. Instead of upgrading to a double level cart, to haul back and forth from school, go make a home-made meal to bring in and enjoy the next day with your favorite coworkers. Use your time in a way that balances things out.

Some of you still will say that idea is absurd. From the top they will say, "There are too many students to have two prep periods." "We can't hire more staff. We have been looking. There is no one." "The budget will not allow it." From the top they will say a whole bunch of things to remind you, that's just the way it is. The idea is not absurd; it is just different. Well beyond English teachers, all teachers need to make sure work is left in the building.

Part of finding balance will feel shaky at first, uncomfortable maybe. You will be guilted by your coworkers and administration, whether they do it on purpose or just out of habit. Trust the process. You may even guilt yourself at first. I did for a while... You will guilt yourself unless you start finding yourself busy with what is supposed to be filling your time outside work. Leave your computer at school, along with that whole cart full of papers, snacks, stickers, and stress. Disconnect your work email from your phone. Hell, throw your phone away too... LOL

Leave it all and start finding time for whatever is on the other side of your

recovery.

This next idea of learning to find balance exists in most jobs,

again. It is probably the hardest pattern to break, because it is in our

minds. In all teaching positions, we take our figurative work home with us

too. Besides planning, grading, phone calls, and emails we do at home,

we spend a lot of time thinking about our jobs. We go home and talk

about what happened at work. We tell the same work story to multiple

people, anyone who will listen really. If we have no one to talk to, it's

even harder to escape the work thoughts running around in a person's

head. At least for me, I used to dwell too much on things from work. Part of the whole social emotional trap exists here too. Everyone we entail with our stories tells us how great we are, even if your spouse does it just to shut you up. Our non- teacher friends (Thank God for them!) talk about anything to move the conversation in another direction. They tell us how patient we must be and how they could never do that. It has some similarities to an abusive, unhealthy, and unbalanced relationship.

In our relationships, instead of asking each other how work was, maybe we can start asking how are you? Maybe instead of responding when someone asks you how the day was, you respond with a story different from work. This will take serious effort again. It is a deep grained pattern.

Some of us have lost our balance terribly. It seems for many, the only thing we know how to talk about is work. We start with the complaints usually. "Guess what happened today?" "Do you know what so and so did?" We then put our poor companion into a coma, talking about people they often have never met!

To help find balance, we need to start talking about life when we are outside of work. Many of us need to create a life outside of work first; a meaningful one! Something we really want to talk about. Even though we spend 33% of the day at work, it needs to become less of our lives. To have any chance of recovery, teachers need to make a conscious effort to talk much less about work when they leave the building. I mean much more than legally in public, or using names, etc. I want to remind you again about FERPA here, and you know damn well you all do it to your own understanding and interpretation of the law. Good teachers care so much about what is happening in that building; it is hard not to talk about outside of work. It seems like a natural part of the teaching gig, but it doesn't have to be.

Teachers need to make a special effort to not bring their students' troubles home with them. Hangout with teacher friends and colleagues that talk about anything else except work. Why? Isn't it good to vent about your feelings? Simply, no, not the way teachers do to one another. Stop venting with coworkers for two very clear reasons. Number one, that gives you a break from the repeated teacher rhetoric of bitching. Number two, talking with people who talk about other things brings diversity into your life and effectively fills your cup. Mothers sharing the construction project of being mothers. Single folks and all their escapades. The Karaoke Kings and weekend DJs. Halftime rap star and the goofiest "adults" telling their most terrible jokes. These are the teachers we should hang out with after work. These are the interactions of a recovering teacher.

In addition, teachers could search for balance by leaving the students' successes at work. Try to consider all student thoughts off, even the good ones. It is just too dangerous a game to let any of those thoughts in. I played the game for a long time, not ever reading the rules or understanding the consequences. There are so many more of your students than your family and friends, it could easily become something you think about more and more. And before you know it, the balance is all thrown off again. It could be overwhelming. It could be a habit that you think makes you a better teacher that is slowly killing you; the you that is not a teacher. *Don't forget, it is okay not to be a teacher all the time.*

Leaving the successes and troubles of students at work may even help you be excited to go to work again. When you can allow your mind to get away from the problems/stressors, it will naturally keep working on them. When you return to those problems at work, the answer may just be sitting there waiting in that freshly restored brain of yours.

Leaving work thoughts at work will keep your cup filled. Of course, there is balance in doing one thing more than another and weighing out your options, but maybe it is much easier. *Balance can be found by simply doing less.*

It's just the same as not talking about too much of your personal life when at work. Of course, the good teacher uses personal life examples to liven up a science lesson or writing prompt. It is okay if your students know a little about your family or personal hobbies. That is a huge part of being a good teacher and making connections. Good teachers know how to open up for the kids, so eventually the kids can open up too. Good teachers need to make sure they don't go too far. Students shouldn't know your family members' names, or which bar you sing Karaoke at on Thursday night. A teacher cannot take too much of their personal lives to work, just the same as they should not take too much work home. There must be efforts made in both directions to find balance. Kind of a push and pull factor thing, combined with simply doing less.

It was my hiking in the woods that enlightened me in this area of balance. I would find myself thinking about students' problems while hiking. I would think about lesson planning or a meeting I had the next week. At the time, I considered myself a better teacher because of this uncontrollable phenomenon. I really thought I was better than others, but really, I was missing out... I was missing out on my hikes!

I caught myself totally unbalanced. I made a real conscious effort to not let school thoughts come into the woods with me anymore. I started making sure to think about my own family. Instead of thinking about what I could do for students, I thought about what I can do for my niece or nephew. How can I help my sister or mom this week? I thought of ways to reconnect with my best friend. I made a real effort to think about my memories with friends and family.

Out on my hikes, I eventually started thinking about my own future. I started focusing more on my own life and setting some personal goals. I started to use my hikes for me, instead of work.

Chapter 10 - Fill Your Cup

I read another part of a book... Thinking back with intention now, I remember why I read only part of it. I had found this book, "How to Teach like A Pirate" on the bookshelf at one of the satellite programs we were supporting. I started reading the book, but like so many others before (especially during the school year), it was not finished.

Each night, I spent so much time studying all the subjects I was teaching as a special education resource teacher. As you recall, I was not much of a student in high school; I could not remember all that stuff, so I needed to freshen up often in many subjects to try to help my students. Some folks, cough cough...general education teachers.... Cough, look at special education as less rigorous or less challenging. Not all, but some.

At least half of general education teachers find fault in special education in my experience. I have seen the ill feeling, more toward other special education teachers than myself, and often warranted for the teacher's numerous downfalls. I have felt the disdain toward myself from real pompous type of general education teachers. The kind of teachers that think what they teach is the most important thing in the world. Just another unhealthy pattern I try to avoid. As noted earlier, there is no accurate comparison between the two teaching niches. It shouldn't matter anyway.

I just wanted to point out I was doing the same thing that general education teachers do. In fact, I was prepping at home for multiple subjects at multiple grade levels. I am certain I am slowly developing ADHD symptoms by trying to be a special education teacher. LOL

All of this was on top of all the paperwork that comes with special education. So let us point out this outstanding similarity and put the other differences aside. What's that some say, comparison is the killer of joy. If this is true, comparison also closes the ears of some. They are too busy pointing out differences to find the point of conversation. And what was the point again here? Oh yes, the book that I partly read because I was too busy after work doing work stuff!

Back to it, I simply never made time to finish the book. I do not want my incomplete assignment to come out as the book was unfinishable though. I am sure the whole thing was worth reading, I just didn't make the time. Each section or chapter, as I remember, was an acronym for PIRATE. One section was P for passion. I was irritability. And I think R was for revenge. A stood for ahoy mate… LOL Something like that.

Okay, I don't recall the rest, but P did stand for passion. Earlier, I mentioned how important it was for me when I brought my personal passion, Bull riding, into the classroom. That idea had been born when reading, "How to Teach Like a Pirate." I was draining at work like usual and on top of that, I was living in a new town by myself. I needed something at the time; I didn't know how important it would become in my own teaching career. This book is where I found one of the most important ways to fill my cup while at work, even amid all my ignorance at the time. The idea has stuck with me, and I interpret it like this.

Introducing personal passion into your classroom can be another, maybe the greatest, way to find balance, and fill your cup, while at work. It is my go-to as a recovering teacher; becoming more and more important the further into teaching I go. So many teachers have passion for their job. As you recall, it was the number one answer to my survey of teachers. But how do we use it?! Do we waste it or use it for future fuel to avoid burning out?

According to Dave Burgess, there are 3 types of passion that should be used in the classroom. Dave says something more that I don't recall exactly, so... In my words, there are three terribly unbalanced passions that are misused by teachers. Our passions are so misguided by the school system swaying our rope, it becomes even more difficult to find footing. I believe if teachers use these 3 types of passion, in a delicate and purposeful balance, we can go well beyond a full cup. If done right, teachers' cups could easily be overflowing.

First, there is the most obvious passion that most teachers have and use. They use this passion to desire the job, jump through hoops to be allowed, and then eventually work the teaching profession. This first passion is the overall idea of helping others. Many public service positions and great people in general, have the passion to help others. They thrive on it. It kind of makes the world go round... I live for it. I love helping people! I don't know why really, but I am sure I learned it from some earth visiting angels along the way.

For teachers, this passion is represented through the desire to help kids. It is the idea that teachers are a critical piece of current society and a little more than just glorified babysitters. This type of passion leads to teachers wanting to reach at least one kid. It is the idea that we plant seeds that we may never see grow, may never be harvested, but we know we play a part in the whole process. It is a fantastic feeling to think you have helped someone have a better future. This passion drives so many teachers to keep pushing on through the paperwork, low pay, and the ever-changing politics year after year. No matter how strong this passion is, it is not enough to get one through.

This first type of passion is a huge part of the social emotional trap. When a public servant, a teacher in this example, thrives on just this one type of passion, it leads to the burnout; it leads to the social emotional catch. This type of passion ignites the fire and is strong! But by itself, this type of passion will not get a teacher through the profession. Quickly, this flame will burn out from overuse.

A second type of passion, according to Burgess, is the passion for teaching the subject. Some teachers absolutely love to teach math. The idea of putting numbers together, sometimes letters, just really does it for them. Other teachers could not live without the language art of back seat driving other people's sentences. In other words, some teachers like to teach English. William Shakespeare whispers from their soul. A graphic organizer is posted on their bathroom mirror, with a highlighter hanging from a string to stress the most important parts of whichever magazine they read while sitting on the toilet. Some other teachers believe they were born into the wrong century and would rather talk about the historical past, no matter how flawed the books they teach from are. I am one of them.

Every teacher has their passion for a particular subject. Mine has somehow become the diverse world of special education, though I feared the whole idea growing up. Who knows? No matter how much this passion exists, it can and does run out as well. There are certain parts of a subject that just don't do it for that teacher, no matter how much they love the subject and try to fake it through.

When I taught history, some of the politics sucked. I am just not into that part of the history curriculum. When I taught math, there's only so many ways to teach the multiplication table with a smile on your face. I came up with some cool action-game-based stuff too. No matter, some parts of teaching math can become a bit redundant after a few years. As a science teacher, I couldn't stand those chemistry equations. I can only handle plugging in so many numbers in one day...

If a teacher tells you they love everything they have to teach in the curriculum, they are lying. We cannot rely on our passion for teaching the subjects we love so much. Just like the one before, it cannot stand alone. Even with the love of helping others and the passion of teaching a subject, a teacher will only go so far.

The 3rd type of passion is the most neglected, in my opinion. It is also the most important! Teachers believe they must get through the curriculum, must make their minutes, must appease the grading rubric to get a job next year. As smart as these folks are supposed to be, teachers may be lacking a bit. Lol. Teachers think that getting a kid to the next grade level is the most important thing in life sometimes.

Some teachers have lost way too much energy focused on what they teach, rather than who they teach. School systems create an environment where the second passion fills the teacher's and the student's time. Schools fill your schedule up with so much "bull shit" to get done, you run out of time for this 3rd type of passion.

This most important tool of a teacher is forgotten or neglected so often. It is sometimes frowned upon by others. The 3rd passion, given to us by Burgess, is a teacher's personal passion.

This is the idea of bringing oneself into the classroom. Personal passion is the part of your life that you bring into the classroom on purpose. Sometimes it is a picture, a song, food, or even a piece of jewelry. Other times, it is your charisma, your jokes, just your good old personality. You bring this personal passion into the classroom to remind you who you are and how strong you can be, well beyond the institution you work for.

For me at one time, this was bull riding. My passion then became hiking, combined with shed hunting. I often use music, like so many others, as a personal passion. It has evolved over the years, and I am sure it will continue just as we do throughout our lives. *What has not changed about my personal passion, is that I bring it into the classroom on purpose, as frequently as needed.* Bull riding posters on the wall with an update each week. Later in my teaching career there were stories about where I saw the last bear or found my coolest rock. I brought the antlers, fossils, geodes, and more to school; I brought nature to them a few times.

I brought a piece of me, a piece of life that so many had never experienced into my classroom. It felt good! It not only did wonders for me, but it also created some good relationships with the kids. It turns out the more you have to give to the students from outside of school, the more they are filled up to give back to you! Passion feeds passion.

I know teachers bring stuff into the classroom. I know they often bring things into the classroom for the students to learn and eat. Boy oh boy, do teachers give kids things to eat. I know some people, me for a while, confuse a personal passion with helping others. We forget to separate passion number 1 from passion number 2. I often used to make the argument, "helping others makes me feel good!" *This is not what this most needed type of personal passion is about. It should be for you alone.*

It should make you excited. Yeah, I'll say it. Forget the students for a second and give yourself a break, make yourself satisfied. If it's food, eat it in front of them to make them jealous.

Give yourself a feeling of outright happiness while at work. Play that country song that they all bitch about, then nod their heads along to, and eventually sing with you by the end of the year. Singing John Denver's, Country Road with a bunch of little thug wannabes, is still one of my favorite memories in all the years of teaching. I have even been lucky enough to make singing with my students a bit of a tradition year after year. Almost releases too much Oxytocin in this old teacher's eyes.

Do it for you! Fill your cup with the things you love the most, no matter what the students think, or what I, or the rest of the teachers in your hall think. Dance like no one's watching. Grow some plants in the corner. Play the ukulele... Lol. Play some phantom of the opera like it's going out of style, read the students your latest poem shot down by the publisher, etc. Do whatever it is that I can't think of right now to get your attention and make fun of you.

Put effort into practicing this passion daily. Do the things that you love outside of work and fill your cup with some personal passion! It is as simple as if you want to care for others, you must first learn to care for yourself. With so many to care for... give yourself special extra attention first!

A little piece of advice on how to fill your cup with passion... find your niche in the teaching world. Your niche should not be decided by others from year to year, based on raises, praises, and promises. Your place in teaching should not be decided by what others say you are good at and need you to be good at for the system. I spent too many years in a niche, because others told me how good I was at it. Reinforced by others' compliments and my own ignorance, I didn't know how to find anything else. Don't make mine and so many others' mistakes your own. That is not just the way it is for you. Find your niche by exploring what makes you happy while at work. There are so many positions in a school. There are so many ways to make a difference. This simple act of looking for yourself will keep your cup from emptying too much.

For students in college thinking about heading in the teaching direction, find a way to diversify your degree. For teachers already in the system, find a way to continue your choice of where you want to be. For teachers to be and seasoned veterans alike, have the confidence to move on and find a better place to work. Never stop learning, kind of thing. Give yourself the option to choose where you want to be. Do not set yourself up to feel stuck in your career. This type of freedom will fill your cup with an additional passion.

I have felt stuck. I have been used for my strengths by schools, with no regard for my own happiness. I have been strongly encouraged and directed by people who needed something. I was made to feel proud of it too. From the principals that needed my specialty, I was sold to believe that I was exactly fit for the part. I really thought I was special, as I was slowly dying inside. I know if I had continued with their plan, I would no longer be a teacher. Their educational/business blend did not match me as a person. It had me stuck in a different way, almost addicted, but hating my career.

Going through the feelings of being stuck and fighting this phase led me onwards. I broke away from those strong patterned currents ruining my career. Realizing and fighting the social emotional nets allowed me further upstream. I said, "no" to all the teaching I had done before and moved out of my comfort zone. I walked away from a renowned district and school, the most money I had made in my career, state retirement money, and what I had always known as a teacher. I found something I had never even knew existed in teaching. It was at this time; I found contract work.

It was working as a contracted teacher that taught me that teaching within your niche can be incredibly important to keeping your cup filled. Contract teaching is not the overall answer; it just helped me at the time. Teaching in a happy place, for me some freedom at the time, might be the most important way to keep your cup filled.

For sure, a contracted teaching position has its downfalls. Eating alone in your classroom. Treated like a redheaded stepchild by some. (No offense to stepchildren and red heads, it's just a saying) Contracted workers are sometimes treated as if you are only halfway in the door and halfway out no matter how hard they work. There are certainly some different hardships that can accompany working as a contracted teacher, but for me it felt right and still feels right. I will continue until it does not feel right. *That is what recovering teachers do; we put ourselves first, knowing that is the only way to consistently help others.*

Working as a contracted teacher first gave me the feeling of freedom, which led to another important aspect of keeping your cup filled. I furthered my understanding of recovering teacher by learning to say "no". I learned how to say no to needy students. I sometimes could squeeze out a no to other teachers in need too. I learned to say no to my own bad patterns. I felt empowered in a certain way by doing less. Working as a contract teacher with this new two letter word made me feel wanted, needed, and most of all in charge. At this point in my career, schools were in desperate need of teachers. I never planned on finding this advantage here; it really found me.

There was one specific event in my contract teaching that showed me what I was trying to believe at the time. The Sped Coordinator of this large district had gathered us around to see how things were going with another new way they had asked us to collect data. This was on top of the other 2 ways that we were effectively collecting data. But according to this district, this year, they needed to appease some lawyers and protect the district even further from "crazy parents". His words. As he went around the table, asking each person how it was going, he finally came to me. He asked the same question, and I responded, "I'm not doing that." "What," he said, as all the faces at the table looked in my direction. I responded. "There is no time left in the day...I am not going to do that." I said out loud in public with confidence, what so many others were saying behind closed doors.

I never did either. He and others asked me in private later. I let them know that as soon as they built that into my schedule, I would get it done. There literally was not time in the day to do it; I was not acting unreasonably. When I later explained to him again, he asked me to do it while teaching, to build it into the class schedule. He wanted me to have the students come to my desk one at a time and input data all day.

That is not how I teach. I am a direct instruction, one-on-one, hands-on activities, monitored student led teaching, walk the room, and create some fun, entertaining type of teacher. I am a good teacher! Ask me to sit behind a desk and input data all day... LOL I calmly explained to him again, "that is when I teach." He had seen me teach; he knew how good I was. He wrote it in my reviews... I stared at him blankly until it was over. It was difficult and uncomfortable, also new to me. But the power of "no" had started.

He went as high as the district special education coordinator to try to get me to budge. They even told on me. They told my contract company, which was a huge mistake. My company was on my side and offered to advocate for me, but I reassured them I had it all under control. Confidence flowed from an overfilled cup...

I explained to the coordinator that my prep is for writing IEP's, meeting with other teachers, planning lessons, printing individual lessons for my 60+ special education students in math, reading, and writing in two different grade levels, because they were down a teacher. (I had offered to do both grade levels and was already getting overtime pay that my company had gotten for me that this very coordinator had signed off on. She knew and she still asked for more!!!)

I continued to tell her prep was to call parents, make copies, and then use the restroom so I could hold it for the next few hours. For the first time in my life, I was so confident in my saying no that there was no other choice for them.

Eventually they looked at everything I was doing and agreed with me, or just appeased me because they had no other choice. I was, *I am too good to be fired*. I don't mean for this to come out as pompous. I just know this as a recovering teacher! My direct supervisor said go ahead and do what you have been doing, but please don't let the other teachers know. LOL Well, damn it, I am letting you know.

Start saying no! You can also say it without an explanation point. A simple no will do too or any other version of refusal. Using the word no does not make you a bad person! It seems so many others, just like me, feel bad when we can't or don't want to do something for someone. It's like a weird type of self-inflicted guilt, I guess.

It was only because I was contracted at the time and had multiple companies contacting me all the time that I felt that new power. What was this desperate school going to do, fire me? Not a chance... I had never needed that power in the past, but now it made me feel invincible.

Every week, just about, another offer would come in. So many schools needed me more than I needed them. Contract work made me feel like a recently dumped man, being hit on constantly by too many beautiful women, or at least decent looking. It felt good! Many times, the new job offered more, but I just wanted to finish out the year with the students I had fallen in love with. I still have a bit of the social emotional trap in me, but with awareness. I can still escape when needing to fill my cup.

Chapter 11 - Teaching Off Trail

Teaching is a lot like hiking if you do both all the time and consider yourself a writer. LOL Though my hiking is most likely not like yours, I am certain the ever-growing population of hikers/teachers can relate a little bit... The hiking I do now is considered dangerous or even unethical by some, maybe by most. It's different than how most hike and equally different from how I grew up hiking. When I was younger, hiking meant driving to a trail head, hiking for a few hours, then returning to the vehicle to go home. As a child, this was all I knew.

Growing up with some wild friends and crazy brothers, we went on hikes here and there too. On family vacations or weekend adventures we made our way into what we thought were the wilds. Even then, it was mostly on well-established trails used by so many strangers before me. Close to the same scenario as that "great discovery" of Christopher Colombus. As a kid, I discovered a whole new world each time I went on a hike.

This fantastic feeling of being outdoors followed me into adulthood, as I made a hobby out of hiking some of the greatest trails throughout America. Little did I know that type of hiking would not satisfy me for long. I needed more than following in other's literal footsteps.

Only in the last 6-7 years, almost in tandem with writing this book, hiking has changed into something much different for me. I rarely hike on a trail and mostly disdain each moment when I am on a trail, near a road, find someone else's boot print, etc. I prefer to be alone and barely handle company, because my hikes are so different.

Quickly, I will tell those of you that I have hiked with, the right company changes that. I will happily have the greatest conversation with a girlfriend, following her up any trail. The views somehow become even more beautiful. I will happily take any of my friends and teach them some of the things I am learning out there. Sometimes, I still enjoy driving to another state and getting on one of those famous trails on the internet, to take turns posing in the same picture found on the internet, by everyone that has already been there... LOL They are new to me, so they are usually worth it, but only once! The hiking that I have fallen in love with is very different and came seemingly out of nowhere.

Somehow, I didn't learn about deer shedding their antlers until I was an adult, around 30 years old. I even hunted deer a little as a kid and still missed out on this information. On top of that, after acquiring the information, I was always too busy with work and bull riding injuries to go try it. Once I did, I fell quickly into an addiction I still practice today. Finding deer and elk antlers in the Az. Mountain country was not an easy thing to learn, and I mostly did it on my own. Everyone seemed so busy with work and such. It was hard to get even my most adventurous friends out a couple times per year. But for me, hunting shed antlers is a must until one day when I can't.

It was this hobby of shed hunting that completely changed my understanding of hiking. It might be changing my whole perspective on life. On some of our adventures as kids, my brothers and I went off trail, of course. We went until we were scared or lost, then made our way back to the truck and then a gas station for snacks. On some deer hunts growing up, we went far up north in Minnesota, but even that was marked with bright pink ribbons to lead you comfortably back to a road. The road would then take you back towards heat and many more comforts. Or at least a few comforts and some warm chili.

My new type of hiking/camping did not have these familiar comforts. Hiking for shed antlers had two simple principles for me; do it where no one else wants to and do it often. I knew if I hiked further and harder than others, I would find what they did not. I knew if I made it harder than others could handle, I would get to those untouched parts of the woods. I made it hard on myself on purpose as I first learned this type of hiking. I still follow some of these principles to this day. There is so much more that goes with this, but obviously when hiking in Elk/Deer country the more you do it and the more places you can get away from where people have already been, the greater success you can have.

Once I started hiking under these new conditions, I realized I needed to approach things a bit differently. Through trial and error, I figured out the best snacks to bring, the lightest tools to have handy, and how much water was needed. I found my favorite brand of hiking boots, preferred hiking clothes, and all the other little things that made me somewhat successful. I planned so much, maybe too much, with the weight of my pack.

I also dealt with the realization that I was not as outdoorsy as I had previously thought. Cabins with comfy beds, campers with generated heat, tents with multiple sleeping bags and pillows, trail hiking away from and then back to the car, and so much more did little to prepare me for this new type of hiking/camping adventure. I had a whole lot to learn. And of course, I am still learning as I continue my shed hunting passion.

One of the first outstanding lessons I learned was weird for me. I dealt with some sensory issues I never knew I had. On my hikes, I would have these random bouts with it. It seemed I could feel way too much. Suddenly, I would notice the swarm of gnats or mosquitoes around my head and then not forget about them for a long while. I could feel them in my ears, the side of my eyes, and any other crevasse they could benefit from my sweat. Even if I sprayed myself with that poison, which I try not to, I could feel them hovering. It truly bothered me to the point where it was ruining my hikes. I let it ruin my hikes. Until I decided not to let it.

When I learned to ignore the bugs, or use the cold weather to avoid them, I could feel the arachnids coming after me. They left their silky strands between every tree and branch out there. All the untouched places I needed to be were only untouched by people. Spiders are everywhere. One morning, broken pieces of web floated in the wind highlighted by the sun rising behind them, mesmerizing. Probably one of the coolest things I have seen. But the feeling of being covered in webs sucked.

On top of that, I would feel the branches scratching at my legs, poking me randomly here and there. I would feel the moisture from the grass slowly saturating my "waterproof" boots. All these cumulated feelings were super annoying and sometimes made my hikes much shorter! *No wonder people hike on trails.* I noticed these things too much. I felt them much more deeply than I needed to. It was a huge learning curve for me and at the time; I thought that was just the way it is, and I didn't know any better.

The next lesson should have been obvious for me, but it still needed to be learned in this whole new world of hiking. I was so goal oriented; I sometimes ruined my own hikes. I talked to myself over and over to the extent that it haunted me. "Hike until you find one", "You need to get 5 total this weekend", "You can't go home until…" I would tell myself all kinds of things. LOL. Even my brother said to me, "Do you think you can ever hike again for fun?" I thought I was having fun.

Looking back, I had become so infatuated with the outcome of the hike that I was missing a whole lot. My goals, though important, were

ruining the adventure. Like Miley Cyrus says, "It's All About the Climb."
There is a whole lot more in between here and there...

With time, I am learning to be less goal oriented and a little less competitive... even with myself. I am trying to learn how to relax. Still, as I retrained this part of my brain, there were new worries following me through the woods. As I let go of thinking about my goals, the new freedom led to some real serious type of fears. The more my mind opened, the more I had to be afraid of.

It also could have been the first rattle snake encounter. Or it could have been that weekend I walked up on a bear and her cubs. I guess it could have been when my knee popped out 3 miles into my hike. There was a lot to be afraid of out there, whether I realized it or not. I had avoided many downfalls already, whether I knew that or not too.

Maybe those other thoughts and feelings I was trying to get rid of were needed. Those great distractions that I had intentionally got rid of kept me from thinking about how dangerous, or at least serious, some of the present situations really were. No matter which side I chose it seems, there was always going to be something lurking in my thoughts. I realized

I needed to find a balance between my own personal issues, freedom, and goals.

There is nothing wrong with having goals. They are an essential part of our lives and the people we can become down the line. In my case, the same goals that I thought drove me were actually blinding me. I had let them take over some essential parts of enjoying a hike that many never even get to experience. My goal driven mentality was the very cause of some of the feelings I really did not need to have while on a hike in the middle of some beautiful places.

Even though some of those goal-based emotions were fantastic and unforgettable when met, the other failures always outweighed them. It was a punishment I didn't even realize I was putting on myself, until I did.

So, I fixed it. I decided I could hike more for the destination and distract myself once again. On my way, of course I would look for shed antlers. My focus however, I could turn into how far I could go, or could I get to the top, or could I get to the bottom… So many places to go. I focused on these other things instead and did well for a while. Some of my earlier struggles with sensory issues/emotions were all together disappearing. Destination hiking, with the attached success of finding sheds here and there, transformed me as a hiker. It helped transform me as a person, really. It felt like it was working. The less I tried, the better.

I could also use destination hiking as an accomplishment when needed. No matter whether I found something or not, at least I got a workout. I could use that success to help me with any failure type emotions, if I did not find what I was looking for. Destination hiking seemed good to me. I almost always could make it where I was going, but then I realized…

I didn't know where I was going. Most important, when it really came down to it, I wasn't going anywhere. No matter what ridge, hilltop, or valley I decided was the finale, I was still lacking. Unless of course, I had found a cool rock or an antler. The truth was, I was always really looking for something.

This, of course, made me think back on my goals again. I was feeling very trapped in this way that I was approaching my own passion-filled hobby, until it all changed.

There was no real moment, just a transition. I have no outstanding story that carried me through to the other side. One day, it just kind of happened. I stopped looking for antlers and they started looking for me. My brother says I am crazy... Some of you will agree with him, but I believe in miracles. I have seen way too many to not believe that the most amazing things can happen. And it turns out the more you believe in miracles, the more you get to experience them.

I started trying a bit less up in my head and miracles were happening. I allowed myself to see and then try something different. I didn't do less hiking, I just slowed down…. As I slowed down, I learned about Geodes in the area. While looking for these beautiful gorgeous little rocks, I found more antlers. One rainy season, I found mushrooms. I found more varieties of mushrooms than I knew existed in Arizona. While looking at all these exotic mushrooms, I found antlers. Then there were flowers and trees that deserved to be photographed, along with animals I had only seen in a zoo or on the internet. I found everything I was not looking for, while still finding my sheds.

I found adventure. I found a way, for me, to love hiking again. I found my own way by not accepting that hiking had to be on the same path as others. Then I found my way by dealing with my own shit and learning a new way to dance with mother nature. All of it had so much less to do with the hike and much more with how I approached it. I am a recovering Hiker! LOL

I hear a lot of people talk about hiking, in addition to seeing their posts, if I have found myself down that rabbit hole... When I make it back from the middle of the forest, nearer to the outskirts, I even run into and talk with other hikers. On top of that, even as seldom as I hike trails, I have noticed some things. There are some evident patterns. As I understand it, hiking is a growing past time of a lot of screen watching, "influencing" or influenced folks. As I have seen it, the trails are filled with people trying to hike like those they have seen on a screen. There are so many in love with the idea, but so blindly exploring an already explored trail.

To me, so many hikers try to hike rather than just do it. Just like my own past misunderstandings, so many of us do too much. We try way too hard in the wrong directions. We buy the best shoes, rate and race the trails, camouflage ourselves to match the trees out of season, and take more pictures than steps.

Some Facebook folks I know, that call themselves hikers, seem mostly there to be seen. Girls all dressed up, phone in hand, sharing with the world before they are even done... My own friends time themselves each weekend on the same trail to the same top. They time themselves week to week, trying to beat their own time, missing all the highlights, simply on goal induced repeat. Of course, they still take the time to snap a bare-chested pic to post to their followers on multiple platforms from the top. Just like I did in my own way, rather than just hiking, we try to do so much more than what is necessary. This is just like teaching.

Somehow as a 10+ year teacher, I didn't know so many things in the teaching world. More like becoming a teacher made me not see so many things. I was blindly following other's pedagogies, lesson plans, textbooks, curriculum, etc. because I was afraid of something different. Or I didn't know anything different.

Eventually teaching became too much like following the trails. I knew only what I had followed, instead of what I had seen. Just like those before me, I was simply following, as if there was no other option. I was so distracted by the designed beauties and the highlighted dangers of the trail itself, to look anywhere else. It took me so long to look left or right, because the path was set out straight in front of me in the most "organized" of ways and everyone was walking that same direction. *I was scared to get lost, not realizing that lost was the exact adventure I needed in my teaching career.*

I have argued with too many that a person cannot plan an adventure. It just doesn't work that way. We plan trips, not adventures. The adventure starts when everything we planned goes wrong. Adventures find us! *If one prepares for an adventure the same way they prepare for life, their very own patterned life will prevent them from the adventure.*

Work can be the same way, no matter how I ran from it early in my career. I didn't think I could find adventure in teaching the way I had done other things in life. Work felt like somewhere between a trip and an adventure at the time; that's just the way it is with behavioral health education. Really, work was simply another annual trip, repeating the same patterns from year to year.

If I wanted more than just a trip each year, it was another view around the bend that I had to go see by myself. I couldn't find freedom and adventure in my teaching by listening to the peers around me either; they were all stuck on trail. There was no one to lean on for this. No one was trying to prepare for an adventure in teaching the way that I was; they were all just trying to get through the trip.

When I went off trail in my own teaching career, of course I ran into some issues. A cloud of them following me, like all those flying bugs of the forest. The first issue being all the things that a responsible teacher can be bothered by. As a self-proclaimed good teacher, I noticed all the things that I used to do and thought about them as if I needed to do them. No matter how I tried to detach from my old ideas and ignore them, they followed me... into the woods. But really there was nothing needing my attention. There was nothing that I could really do to deal with all the extras.

Most of those emails can be deleted, without even a scan. They just don't matter. Also, it turned out if you do not pay attention at those meetings that you say don't matter, you don't miss out. There are also a handful more things which you get to decide, that do not deserve your full attention. Teaching responsibilities include a whole lot of stuff that does not matter. *Just like the bugs of the forest, it was my decision to not let work bug me.*

Going off trail, whether literally or in teaching, goes in many directions obviously. Once you leave the trail, how do you know which direction to go without getting lost? Are you learning what hallway to avoid on your campus? Do you know what meeting to fall asleep at or even skip? Do you know what staff you should say good morning to and move on from, so you don't get stuck? Have you mastered the art of small talk without really spending too much patience, energy, or willpower? Hell, do you even work at the right place, or are you stuck?

On the other hand, have you learned which staff fill you up and make you want to be there? Have you learned how to be friendly without trying to be friends with everyone?

Learning the right path to walk is what helped me the most in the woods. I needed to go through the thorns, just like the Elk before me, to find their fallen antlers. I didn't need to go back that same way. Some hills and cliffs were going to lead to nothing... It didn't mean I had to see that as a failure. There were some great plants to look at, rock structures to climb, and beautifully sung bird songs to listen to on the way. Similarly, learning the right path to walk at school has kept me going happily and confidently.

We teachers dwell on goals and good feelings a lot! And then teachers are trained to get high scores, based on the high grades of their students, based on bullshit curriculum. We crave to be better and more than we are. As a teacher it feels good the more people that "need you", like you, want you to be there, etc. – it becomes part of the drive. Teachers are so goal driven toward the top, we learn to fight for elevation rather than find another, better, different way. Another better "trail" is often lower in elevation than where we are trained to look. The top is not the only place where magic exists. I have learned that the top is a distracting destination. It is fun to visit and rewarding in a sense, but most of the greatest interactions are somewhere between the bottom and the top. I know for me to find the adventure I want as a teacher; I need to avoid the top as much as possible.

I don't do it as much anymore, but I hope I am not the only worried teacher out there. It seems to me, so many teachers are worried about getting into trouble. Trouble from administration, parents, or even students now a days. Trouble for being late, trouble for forgetting, trouble for anything they can think of. Some teachers are even worried about getting fired for some crazy reason. I am not talking about terrible people that should get dismissed. I speak of great hard working, self-minded, achieving people worried about getting fired. I really don't understand the unwarranted fear or where it comes from.

These same worried people are stuck with my stories from the woods year after year. What about bears? What if you get lost? What if? *There are too many negative endings to what if questions.* In a couple of million steps, on hundreds of trips and dozens of adventures, I have experienced the following. I have seen 6 rattle snakes, 3 that were close enough for me to be super thankful to avoid. I have seen close to a dozen bears that all ran off in the other direction. I was lucky enough to stumble on a few mountain lions that did the same thing. And once was startled to death by a pinecone falling right next to me as I was eating a snack. There are circumstances in the woods that we should be prepared for but never worry.

Without making up fears and distractions, along with ridding ourselves of self-inflicted crippling choices, there are so many miracles available out there. I don't want to talk you into hiking like me, there is too much competition already. In fact, please stay on your trails when it comes to hiking. But when it comes to teaching, get off trail! There are so many miracles available in the teaching career too.

Chapter 12 - Fill Your Cup Again

You Need It

When I started writing this book, I didn't know exactly where I was going with it. The idea kept evolving and the words just kept flowing. The words poured out like a leaky faucet. The kind that drips through the night and starts to get annoying unless you do something about it. I realized many times throughout the writing process I was trying to prove my point. I was trying to rebuttal all the questions that were sure to come. I was trying to win an argument that wasn't even there yet, though I knew it would come. It goes back to the whole thought about me avoiding using statistics in this writing. It is a back-and-forth seesaw, with anyone who is bored enough to ride, that really is no fun for me and goes nowhere. A waste of time...

I tried to stay away from the need to "win an argument." Overall, I avoided those so easily fudged numbers to try and focus on the feelings of those I spoke with, the patterns of stories, the repeated offenses that were felt year after year. I really wanted to focus on the opinions and patterns of so many teachers, that seemingly were becoming facts.

I decided to take quite a bit out of the book in the editing process, based on this attempt to really create focus on the recovery. I had gone too much into my own experience and other's paid for opinions spurted out as statistics. I did not want to create a competitive comparison and lose the focus of readers. I do think my experience as a teacher is diverse and unique. That, along with my own hobbies and who I am as a person has led to this perspective. I can look around at any school and see how different I am from others. Nevertheless, here I go again trying to prove myself.

It was my weird journey that led to identifying the first step to recovery. Same as in chapter 10. Teachers need to find their niche asap. But how? As mentioned, teachers in this book refer to ALL of those involved in the process. I watch so many teachers complain about their job, even talking about quitting year to year, but never leaving. It seems so many know they don't want to be where they are, but don't know how to go anywhere else. I watch so many become stuck until they eventually burn out. I luckily avoided this due to my unique position at first. I worked in many different school environments without having to leave a job to get this diverse understanding.

I then worked in different jobs by leaving, by saying no, and not following the puppet strings and half-assed promises. I found confidence with so much less care about what my colleagues, what so many call family, thought about me.

I found confidence from riding bulls first, not teaching. I learned confidence in my hobby that helped me in my job. While overcoming the instinctive fear, I learned to move on top of that beautiful animal, not bear down to fight something you cannot outpower. Get forward. Shove your hips. Sit up straight. Keep moving! I became a better rider by not getting stuck.

I became a better teacher by not becoming glued down to one location too. I was able to experience so much by not getting stuck in my teaching career. I found my niche in teaching by not fighting the system, instead using it. I found where I wanted to be by not settling. Find a happy place in teaching anyway you must, whether that is following the Applebee's man out or strategically moving within the profession.

I have found my niche in contract teaching. First, I found contract teaching for larger companies. In the long run, even that was not specific enough for me. That is, until I need to use it again. They still have my number, and I hear from them often. Second, I found contract teaching for a smaller company run by my past work acquaintances/friends. By learning to move on, I have found some great people to work with again, who trust each other, communicate with each other, build each other up, and leave each other alone. I will remain with this team as long as it fits me. I will stay as long as they accept me as a recovering teacher.

I am not against public schools. There are great social aspects found in public schools that will not be available in other forms of teaching. The sports and other extracurricular activities found in public schools are spectacular compared to most smaller institutions. Public school teaching is just not for me anymore.

I am not opposed to charter schools either, though there are some shady patterns popping up over the years. Because I am contracted with these companies it is easier for me to ignore the political shade casted down from above. No matter... Charter schools serve a great purpose for students who do not like that public realm, just like me. I enjoy contract working within the charter school system, traveling during the week. I literally do not have to sit in the same classroom day in and day out or in the identical school building year after year… Most importantly, *I feel less stuck.*

I have not had the chance to work at a Montessori type school, but that sounds sweet. Let the students figure out, based on a bunch of cool projects and questions. That's kind of what I do when I know administration isn't watching. LOL Hell, that's what I do for fun at home.

As a non-parent, I do not know much about home schooling. But I was an older brother to 2 younger siblings and an uncle to some nephews and nieces. I like teaching others at home however we want to. Memorizing the multiplication table while bumping a volleyball back and forth. Or discussing topics for an argumentative essay, while working out with my nephews. Learning while having outright fun in any way we wanted, because we weren't at school with all those stupid rules. LOL

Teaching and learning are interesting to me; it's outright fun when you learn to do it right. I am obviously a teacher at heart and with all the options out there, I can remain one.

This book is not against any healthy style of teaching. All these options are out there so you can find your niche as a teacher. Find the arena that allows you to make teaching fun again. Find a job that doesn't

just drain you; find the one that sends you home with a fuller cup.

Earlier I discussed the social emotional benefits that can become a

type of trap. It can make a teacher feel like they can save the world.

Giving breakfast to a hungry kid, staying late to tutor a struggling student,

crying with a young lady that lost her mother can surprisingly make a

person feel good. Not at the moment, of course. There is just this great

feeling that you could be there, doing something more than simply

shoving curriculum into their brains. I cannot stress enough how tricky

and enticing this trap can be... it is an easy one to caught up in.

After you find your niche, teachers need to know when and how

to create boundaries. Teachers need to pay attention to their own social-

emotional feelings when they go home at night. They need to turn

"school" off when they leave the building. Some teachers need to go

home and give their families every social emotional feeling they have left.

Damn it! I slipped again and it will happen to you too. Even there

in writing this, I say go home and give... This idea needs to become the

opposite. Give every ounce in your cup to those you love at home before you go to work and after work. This will take incredible attention on your part. There are way more faculty and students than there are your family and friends. Except for maybe you weirdos that include Facebook and Instagram friends. Yes, that is a loud hint that you should not fill your cup with your phone; that is just another mirage that is draining so many cups nowadays. Get off your phones and start giving life a little bit more. It will take a mighty effort to leave work at the door and start thinking about yourself, but if I can do it, so can you.

As I say that I know some of you are thinking, "Well that's what I do. I am a teacher. That's what we do. Some of the kids have nothing else. If I don't do it, who will?"

Okay, first, then stop complaining about it! Don' walk around and pollute my beautiful air with your negative words. Suffer in silence if you are choosing such a difficult path. And second, no!!!! Do it all day and do it your best but turn it off at the door. I am not saying turn into an asshole. I am not saying to become a bad worker either. Turn it off for the kids at your work; turn it on for your friends/family. *Experience the miracle that can fill a cup by drinking from another spring*!

Find the balance. There really is another way. This idea that I am still practicing is almost impossible to discuss, without sounding like a burnout or a bad teacher. It is complicated to explain because I am still learning it. It is so difficult to put into words because it is something you must feel.

For me, it was doing math with my niece and showing her more pride than I do with my students. And I did it on purpose. It was the smile I put on my own family's face, rather than an annual stranger. We continued to get her grades up and then make the volleyball team. I had done that for students many times, but never had I used this power so much for my family.

I felt the call of recovering teacher when my older brother called me out for not making the time to take his second child to workout. I had preached to him so much about this book that he found me getting sucked back into the system, too busy with work. I love and hate my older brother for this. *I love and hate him more often now as a recovering teacher.*

I took my nephew to work out, and we still do our best to meet twice a week. This "shoulder time" has been incredibly important. My nephew and I talk about things that people that hangout talk about. I have always done that with students because I spent so much time and effort at work. Now I felt it with my own kin. I realized something. Turns out, it is easy to stop thinking about work when you purposefully surround yourself with the right goals and the right people.

Personally, it was taking a few days off and not feeling guilty about it, that led me to this feeling of recovery. I spent every one of those days not thinking about work. Along with not using my time for work, I thought about everything and everybody else. I even selfishly thought about myself! LOL. It even felt weird when I returned to work the next week. I really, truly felt strange. "Like where am I, kind of thing. Can I do this? What is my password?" In my 15 years of teaching, I had only once or twice before, in all my career, taken a full week off. Taking time off on purpose, for myself, has become something I am trying to make into a new pattern.

I found more recovery when a student asked me why I was smiling all the time. Even more recovery came from working in my niche of teaching, with coworkers who fill my cup. A different type of teaching will feel foreign, but it can be real. Many in the profession think we are better teachers because we go home and cry, think about, plan for, and buy stuff for "our kids." They are not "your kids", "our kids", etc. Call them what you want, but they are your students. There were a whole lot of things I had to stop doing to start smiling. I found recovery by being less like a teacher. LOL! Try not to take this as a negative comment...

You are more than a teacher. *Your JOB is teaching, no matter how proud and great it can make you feel*. Now follow me. This job provides a skill set for you; an incredible skill set that many other professions cannot create. This means as a teacher, walking through the real world, you are gifted with some great skills. I don't think a teacher should turn this off when leaving work.

Use those talents for the real world. Use those one-of-a-kind teacher gifted skills to notice who needs help at the grocery store. Use that teacher gifted expertise to create an open-ended intimate discussion at the dinner table with your family, not about school. Use those incredible, unique skills when you see the opportunities. Look for those teaching opportunities if you really need to be that much of a teacher. Use your job to be a better person outside of work; not to literally do your job outside of work.

Next, use those amazing teaching talents for yourself. Maybe use those skills for yourself first! Either way, use your great patience, attention to detail, organization, hard work, and multi-tasking genius for yourself occasionally. You ever give yourself rewards for your hardships or give yourself a break/timeout when needed? When was the last time you were giving, loving, and caring for yourself? We teachers do it every day for the students.

Each afternoon, practice leaving the students' problems at that school door. Do something for yourself on the way home. Give yourself a golden star for your workout at the gym. And after yourself, compliment your significant other for making a great meal, even if it isn't. (You know, like you do for your students) Then catch up on your own paperwork! The next morning you can start thinking about the students again. I promise, those problems will still be there.

The last repeated rebuttals I can already hear coming from you; "Do you know how many things I have come up with for my students after work hours?" "My best lesson plans come when I am in the shower." (That's weird) "My head is only clear at the end of the day."

"That is the only time to grade." I get it, I get it... there is too much for you to do... Well, *that is only because you are trying to do too much.*

To all of you, I confidently say you are still stuck in the "That's just the way it is" mentality. You still think you must spend all that extra time to be the best teacher you can be. Using more time for work is not the answer. It is what we do outside of work that matters most.! I hope that being the best teacher always comes second to the things that matter most.

I hope that we try to be the best brother, sister, mother, father, son, daughter way before work. I wonder what would happen if we tried to be the best teammates, friends, neighbors, bull riders, etc. before teaching. I could easily make that list longer, and so could you if you stopped wasting your time on work! I hope you get the point. *In case you didn't there is a whole lot more in life than your JOB, as a teacher.* All our jobs make us forget this by filling our minds with too much stuff. It is part of the system we may be stuck in. In my opinion, teachers forget it the most... You are much more than a teacher! In my stronger opinion, without yelling, if we become better brothers, sons, daughters, mothers, etc. we will naturally become better teachers.

Another big reminder of this proposed solution is as simple as the 2-letter word, NO. I need to stress this again and again and again! We, as teachers, are terrible at this in our herd mentality. It is so much easier to follow the asshole in front of you, when following so close. LOL Teachers need to say "no!" Teachers should refuse to do all the extra stuff that is too much. We need to say "no" to the extra meetings and training courses about stuff already discussed. We can personally give less attention to things that will be only implemented for one year and then changed. Say "no" to all those things we complain about all the time; you know what I am talking about, the "stupid stuff."

Teachers also need to say "no" to the other teachers who just make their day harder. This one is tough for me, because I want people to like me... But it is okay to skip having lunch with Ms. Gossip, Mr. Talk Too Much, and Mr. Complain. Complaining about your job is no good for your cup. No matter how good it feels, talking shit never fills a cup. The biggest one I learned to avoid was Mr. Talk Too Much. Listening to nonsense spurted by the ignorant empties the cup quickly. It is okay to not be friends with everyone at work. Be friendly of course but learn how to not allow these types of people to take up too much of your day.

It is okay to say "no" to the students too. They are a constant source of your draining cup, especially when you go above and beyond too often. Don't be like me and play basketball with the kids at recess and then skip your workout with your family, because your knee is sore. Don't make my mistake and check on the student's behavior at lunch for your IEP notes and then not call your sister after work to see how she is doing. Don't be like me and say yes simply because you think it makes you a better teacher. Like a good parent, a teacher must learn to say no. Using the word "no" to students does not only fil your cup, but helps the student grow up.

Administrators may need to learn this word the most; not the way they usually use it, going toward teachers. Administrators need to say "no" to parents and the schoolboard's stupid ideas that make no sense in the day-to-day teaching. Leaders need to say "no" going up. When leaders fail to use the word, then teachers need to say" no" to those leaders.

Teachers need to say "no" to the "stupid stuff" and say yes to time spent helping kids grow up. Do the things that help kids become better people each day to the next; it is that simple. We need to say yes to all that matters to keep our cups overflowing into our students' real needs. I could go on and on about this, but you must decide where the "yes" and the "no" belong to find your own balance. You will feel it as it happens.

Teaching can be so different for everyone. Franklin Habit said, "On teaching...the job seems to require the sort of skills one would need to pilot a bus full of live chickens backwards, with no brakes, down a rocky road through the Andes while simultaneously providing colorful and informative commentary on the scenery." Well said Franklin, but I see it a little more in depth and in many areas well beyond teaching.

As I felt the change in my teaching career, I wondered if this idea of recovering from teaching could be taken into some other areas in my life. First and foremost, driving. Now that I wasn't thinking of teaching all the time, including during my drive to and from work, I was pissed off at traffic. I noticed how many people speed with no intention. I noticed how drivers intentionally speed and slow to screw with one another. I was so obsessed with how terrible people treat others while hidden in their vehicles. I wanted to see if I could use my new learned skills to avoid the stress that I was creating on my daily commute back and forth from work.

I knew many of my habits had been ingrained into me since I started driving. I figured it would take just as much work to recover as a driver as it did in teaching.

I was an anxious, nervous driver when I first started out, especially for that test. It was nerve racking trying to make sure everyone was satisfied by my driving. I thought about all the traffic laws and all the things that could go wrong. I thought about those in my car, well, because you can't help it when they are screaming, air braking, or back seat driving in a filibuster style. Just kidding, but you know how passengers can be when you are first starting to drive. I wanted to impress or at least satisfy everyone in my car.

On top of that, I couldn't help but think about the cars around me and especially behind me. I felt like I had to drive to make others happy, or at least not mad at me. I felt scared sometimes for no reason, or at least anxious. Because I was new to driving, I felt I had to do it just like everyone else. I drove for others rather than myself, but well beyond just the responsible way. New teachers are quite similar.

As a driver, I have never been much of a speeder. I have sped, of course, and I go over the speed limit by 5-8 m.ph. on the highway and the interstate when it's wide open, but I don't speed habitually. I don't ride on people's asses who are obviously stuck behind another vehicle. I don't zigzag back and forth from lanes to cut in front of other cars, just to get stuck at the same light as those I passed. The funny thing is most of these people are not late, there is no emergency. They simply need what feels like instant gratification in doing. Without looking ahead, they pass without purpose, speed up just to break, and never take the time to look at the outcome. These types of drivers can never learn because they never take the time to see the patterns that they are stuck in. They are blinded by their own patterns and cannot learn from their mistakes. This is so many teachers.

You know when that person in front of you takes a bit too long to start driving when the light turns green? How about that driver who swerves into your lane, that has not been drinking? You look over and you see the digital culprit, cell phone in the driver's hand. The next time you stop at a light don't pick your phone up. Is this you, like so many others? I am fighting the habit right now. Look at the vehicles around you. More than half of your NASCAR partners, the ones who passed you a minute ago, will have their cell phone in hand. The short, usually less than a minute break from driving through the rat race is filled with the phone. How could these drivers ever know to look for something different? They never allow themselves the time to reflect. This is just how many teachers go through their careers, not knowing how to recover and ever break away; simply distracting themselves through it all.

Of course there are some good drivers out there too. Drivers who obey the law to the T. I once sat at a broken light for 15 minutes. It was late at night, with no one around. I couldn't get myself to turn. Finally, I took that deep breath and ran that broken red light. Of course, nothing happened. Another time, after a concert, with a truck filled with loud, drunk, older friends I got stuck trying to turn left. I was a sober young driver for my older brother and his crew. I was super nervous with hundreds of other drivers around me. I was still so young and worried about what others thought. The drunk idiots in the back telling me what to do didn't help either. This is the early career of many teachers, feeling unneeded stress trying to be perfect workers and listening to a bunch of drunk idiots. LOL

I guess I drive a little more like a tortoise than a hare. It seems everyone thinks I drive too slowly, including my passengers and definitely the asshole behind me. I am never below the speed limit at a ridiculous rate and yet I am passed often. Not just by younger, wild, speed demons. Older folks pass me too. I am talking about the age you assume don't see as well, may have slower reaction times, and such, they pass me! I am often passed by middle aged women with a phone in one hand and an angry face (probably a stressed-out teacher). I am passed by the same short-sighted angry person over and over because they drive so stupidly. This is most teachers. I only see this because I decided to "slow down." The same as I did in my teaching career, I simply did less to fix my driving.

I try to drive in a way that gets me away from everyone. It turns out if you drive closer to the speed limit, many times the rest of the traffic speeds up and hangs out ahead of you. All congregated together riding their brakes. It gives me time to watch the light and decide to speed up or slow down. When I go up north for my hikes, I leave the house so I can drive at 2-4 in the morning. There is less of that traffic to stress me out in the wee morning. It's a great start to the trip, always. I have gone to the extent of trying to get contracted jobs that are west of my home, specifically for the drive. I do this so I do not have to drive toward the sunrise in the mornings and the sunset in the evenings. It had bothered me for so many years, so I changed it. Less stress. I try to

contract close locations too, so I don't have to deal with other drivers as

much.

I am learning to break my driving patterns, like other patterns I

am fighting in life. I need to see the traffic around me obviously, but I do

not need to feel it. I am learning to try to drive for the lights like any good

driver has learned. (There are not many) When you drive for the lights

you skip all the sit and wait, you avoid all the groups of stressed-out

phone zombies. Driving to hit the green lights allows you to move more

slowly, but more effectively. It makes me think too. It allows a good

driver to notice the sunrise behind them on the drive to work and the

sunset in the rearview mirror on the way home. Me personally, I try to

make sure my drive includes me singing like no one is listening or

watching. This type of transportation allows a person to feel good no

matter what the traffic looks like. This is what a recovering teacher looks

like in traffic.

This is me as a recovering teacher. Daily practices, in all areas of

life, help me make it more consistent in my teaching career. I am healthier in body and mind. More family oriented. More "in tune." I smile more, both in and out of work. I take time to stop working and become more friendly with some of my great colleagues, share life stories rather than work stress. I do not try to impress anyone anymore, except the students, when they need that motivation, empathy, love, listening ear, and so much more. I work for the things I believe in, that build me up, and I am actively learning to ignore the rest that cannot be controlled.

I have become more of what I remember myself as when I was younger. Before teaching. Remember, I accidentally became a teacher through some weirdly connected circumstances. I was not meant to be a teacher, at least not the cookie cutter kind built up from a screwed-up system. I worked hard to dig that hole for myself and now I am working even harder climbing out. I have worked my ass off trying to climb out.

I now make time for my side business, which guess what... includes me hiking. I intentionally spend time being myself, not worried about trying to become a better teacher. I am trying to be a better me. I am happier about my future as a person and an educator. I am a recovering teacher!